FAITH &
RELIGION
IN A SECULAR
SOCIETY

FAITH &
RELIGION
IN A SECULAR
SOCIETY

CARDINAL
JOZEF DE KESEL

Archbishop of
Mechelen-Brussels

Paulist Press
New York / Mahwah, NJ

Cover design by Sharyn Banks
Book design by Lynn Else

English translation by John Alonzo Dick. Copyright © 2022 by Paulist Press.

Originally published as *Foi et religion dans une société moderne* © 2021 by Éditions Salvator. Foreword copyright © 2022 by John Alonzo Dick.

Library of Congress Cataloging-in-Publication Data
Names: De Kesel, Jef, author.
Title: Faith and religion in a secular society / Cardinal Jozef De Kesel, Archbishop of Mechelen-Brussels.
Other titles: Foi et religion dans une société moderne. English
Description: New York / Mahwah, NJ : Paulist Press, [2022] | "Originally published as Foi et religion dans une société moderne, 2021 by Éditions Salvator. | Summary: "Faith and Religion in a Secular Society outlines the great challenges of the Church in modern society with a spirit of synthesis and clarity that make its message very accessible"— Provided by publisher.
Identifiers: LCCN 2022030100 (print) | LCCN 2022030101 (ebook) | ISBN 9780809156221 (paperback) | ISBN 9780809187836 (ebook)
Subjects: LCSH: Church. | Catholic Church—Doctrines. | Christianity and culture. | Christianity and other religions. | Secularization.
Classification: LCC BX1746 .D33513 2022 (print) | LCC BX1746 (ebook) | DDC 230/.2—dc23/eng/20221011
LC record available at https://lccn.loc.gov/2022030100
LC ebook record available at https://lccn.loc.gov/2022030101

ISBN 978-0-8091-5622-1 (paperback)
ISBN 978-0-8091-8783-6 (e-book)

Published by Paulist Press
997 Macarthur Boulevard
Mahwah, New Jersey 07430
www.paulistpress.com

Printed and bound in the
United States of America

CONTENTS

Contents

FOREWORD

CARDINAL JOZEF DE KESEL has been arch-bishop of Mechelen-Brussels, and primate of Belgium, since 2015. A pastoral theologian, with a doctorate from the Gregorian University in Rome, he was professor of theology at the Catholic University of Leuven in the early 1990s, and then responsible for the formation of pastoral workers in the Diocese of Ghent for nearly twenty years.

I remember very well his 2010 widely publicized observation about mandatory priestly celibacy: "I think the Church must ask itself the question of whether it is appropriate to keep the mandatory character of celibacy. We could say that there are celibate priests, but that people for whom celibacy is humanly impossible should also have the chance of becoming priests." Five years later in November 2015, when he became archbishop of

Mechelen-Brussels, Christopher Lamb observed in the *Tablet* that while the bishop of Antwerp, Johan Bonny, had called for the recognition of same-sex marriage, the newly appointed Archbishop Jozef De Kesel called for universal human respect, no matter what one's sexual orientation, because it is "a value that the Gospel shares with modern culture."

In an early interview in December 2015, a reporter asked the newly installed Archbishop De Kesel if he was more progressive than his predecessor, Archbishop André Léonard. "That I am more progressive than Archbishop Léonard I dare not say," he replied. But then he continued: "I do know that as a Church we have to respond to what engages society."

Pope Francis made Jozef De Kesel a cardinal in the consistory of November 19, 2016. Then in December 2017, he was appointed to the Dicastery for the Laity, Family and Life. In 2019, he was appointed to the Pontifical Council for Culture. It was a very appropriate appointment, considering the cardinal's keen interest in faith and culture.

What I so greatly appreciate in Cardinal De Kesel's most recent book, *Faith & Religion in a Secular Society*, is his deep commitment to Christian belief rooted necessarily in contemporary culture.

He is clearly a realist about the situation of the Church today. Most importantly, however, he is a well-informed, hopeful, and positive realist. He understands that the Church must listen to what contemporary people are saying and asking. And he knows that the Church can indeed creatively respond. Cardinal De Kesel's book is refreshingly optimistic.

Dr. John Alonzo Dick, historical theologian,
Leuven (Louvain)

PREFACE

ANYONE WHO COMPARES the situation of the Church and faith from just a few decades ago will see how fundamentally the reality has changed. And that in a span of barely two generations. Of course, these changes started much earlier. They have deep roots in the past. Christianity itself is part of the origin of this evolution within Western culture. But it is as if we are only now really becoming aware of it and realizing how irreversible it is. In the immediate aftermath of the Second Vatican Council (1962–1965), we still knew a great momentum of hope and renewal. Not that this is completely gone today. Pope Francis is doing everything he can to remind us of that. The enthusiasm is still there, but it is tempered; and it is not without questions.

The Council took place more than half a century ago. Meanwhile, the sense of life in Western society has become very secular. It largely determines the zeitgeist in which we live. What will the future bring? What does this mean for the Church's mandate and mission in such a changed society? And above all, how exactly should we understand this process of change? All of this is what I want to reflect on. In addition, for a long time, it hasn't been just about the Church. Due to the presence of Islam in Western society, religion as such has become a subject of social debate.

This book consists of two parts. In the first part, I try to understand the changed situation. Of course, an analysis of the situation itself offers no solutions. But it is certainly important that one assess the situation correctly and that one tries to understand the times in which one lives. This is precisely so that one does not slip into any illusions or take unhelpful paths. What has been the case for centuries is today no longer: the Church no longer lives in a religious and Christian society. For some, that is why the Church has fallen into crisis and confusion. They believe that the Church must do everything it can to turn the tide. That is not our conviction.

The fact that the Church is in crisis is correct. The fact that it is gradually coming to its end in this situation is not correct. But then, the Church has to learn to understand the signs of times and accept the changed situation. The Church will therefore also have to reconsider its mission and reposition itself. I will try to demonstrate that this is not only desirable but also possible, and that it can be entirely situated within the context of a modern secular society. And this without having to conform to all the evidence and argumentation of a secular culture.

I want to reflect about this Church repositioning theologically in the second part of the book. Right at the end of the nineteenth century and into the early twentieth century, the Church openly opposed modern culture. The Church could not conceive itself in a culture that was not or no longer Christian. The Second Vatican Council has really been a turning point here. Better knowledge of the biblical and patristic tradition has opened avenues for a more accurate understanding of the Church's mission and its relationship to the world and society. This is the path I wish to pursue. I want to show that the Church can be completely situated within the context of a secular and modern society. The Church's mission is not to conquer the world, let alone make that world a Church itself. We will distinguish between evangelization and a Christianization of society. Surely, it cannot be the mission of the Church to eliminate other religions and beliefs. Respect for the other, including his or her faith or belief, and interfaith dialogue have also become fundamental values for the Church. It is within this dialogue that the proclamation of the gospel must and can happen.

No, it is not the mission of the Church to conquer the world. However, the Church is called, according to the words of the Second Vatican Council, to be *sacramentum mundi*, the sacrament for the world: the sign of God's love, not only for the Church but for the world. The world that the gospel itself testifies to that God loves it to the very end. I want to help people understand how in this situation the Church in its deepest being is missionary and how God has called it to make known to all God's love, which God showed us in Christ. But it is averse to any urge of proselytism and respects other religious traditions and philosophies.

PART I

UNDERSTANDING THE SITUATION

For many centuries, here in the West, Christianity and the biblical Christian tradition have, to a large extent, determined and shaped culture and society. Church and faith were a simple fact of life. No one questioned religion's place in society. Religion as such belonged to the culture. But today, change has come, slower than we often think, because it has to do with the transformation of the culture itself. That is always a lengthy and complex process.

But it is as though we are only now really understanding that a page has been turned and there is a past that is definitely behind us. Of course, we already knew for some decades that the times have changed, especially in the years of preparation for the Second Vatican Council and the years that have followed. But the origins of that change go back much further in history. In the days following the Council, we still had the impression that the aggiornamento of the Church and its openness to the world would once again ensure an important place for the Church in society. We now know that this has not been the case. A fundamental change has taken place in Western culture itself that inevitably has consequences for the place and the presence of the Church in society.

In short, it comes down to this: Western culture has evolved from a religious to a modern secular culture. Within such a changed culture, religion no longer has the obvious meaning nor the place it used to have. And so the question: What is the meaning and the place of faith and religion in modern society? Do they still have a place or do faith and modernity exclude each other? And if the latter is not the case, what does it mean to be Church and Christian in this changed situation? I want to reflect on those questions.

The cultural change has indeed brought a crisis to the Church. But everything depends on how one should understand that crisis. Should one regret it? Accept it as simply a *fait accompli*?

Or engage in a counterattack? Most importantly, what does the proclamation of the gospel mean in that changed situation? How should the Church be present in society? I want to think about that. I do it in the spirit of a realism that has no illusions, but also in a spirit of faith and with great confidence.

My primary focus here is on Christianity and the situation of the Church. But in many respects, my thoughts are perhaps relevant to the presence of every religion in our society. And that presence of other religions has indeed become a fact of life. Our Western culture is not only in the evolution from a religious to a secular culture. Due to immigration, this secular culture has been confronted with an increasing presence of non-Christian religions. Since Judaism has always existed within Western culture, I am thinking here especially about Islam. Paradoxically, our so-called secularized society is becoming more and more multireligious. If we ask the question about the place of religion in our society, then it's not just for the sake of the secularized context. It is partly due to the presence of Islam that this question is the subject today of both social and political debate.

The question about the meaning and place of religion in our modern society must deal with the question of the growing presence of Islam. Inevitably, this is not only a question about the future of Islam, but also about that of Christianity itself here in the West. That question, too, will increasingly ask, What does the presence of Islam in our regions mean for the Church and for its presence in society? For being Church in a homogeneous Christian society is one thing. Being a Church and proclaiming the gospel in a society where another highly respectable faith tradition is present is another. The question of what the presence of other religions means for the proclamation of the gospel we will address in the second part of this book.

1

Confrontation with a Secular Culture

I N A LONG AND COMPLEX process, Western culture has evolved from a religious Christian to
a secular culture. It was inevitable that the place
itself and the meaning of Christianity were questioned. There are those who say that all this
should not be exaggerated. In the course of its
history, the Church has also experienced other
crises and faced enormous challenges. Just think
of the proclamation of the gospel by Jesus himself and of the first evangelization of the apostles.
Nothing guaranteed their success—if success can
be spoken of at all! Let us also think of the great
crisis of the early developing Church when it had

to make the decision to address non-Jews. Think of the fourth century and the crisis of Arianism when the Church was in danger of losing its own identity. Think of the Reformation and the crisis of modernism that so divided the Church.

It is often thought that the Church has always known crises and has always overcome them. The first is true; the other is not. In the third and fourth centuries, at the time of Cyprian and Augustine, North Africa was one of the most Christian areas. A few centuries later, almost nothing was left of it. Jesus did indeed say of the Church, "The gates of Hades will not prevail against it" (Matt 16:18). But he didn't say where! It is not because the Church has been established somewhere that it will naturally continue to exist there. The Church does not escape historical contingency. So there are crises and challenges that should not be taken lightly.

The fact that the Church has also experienced crises in the past in no way relativizes the crisis we are experiencing today. Moreover, the crisis we face today is something unique and something the Church has never known before. It is the first time that it faces this challenge. Before the rise of modernity, the legitimate right of religion would never have been questioned. In the period of antiquity, the Church proclaimed the gospel in a culture and society where religion had an obvious place. That is not the case with us today.

Today it is not, at least not first, about confrontation with another religion, let alone Islam. What matters is that the Church is confronted with a culture that states that religion is an optional matter. It is not excluded that religion may have some significance for the private life of the citizen, but that does not apply to the development of culture and society. That is, of course, a huge challenge. Hence the crisis of the Church.

Nevertheless, we must be wary of understanding the word *crisis* only in its purely negative sense. It is through crises that the Church grows and learns to understand its mission. Crisis does not necessarily mean that the Church is doing badly. Or, as some argue, that Christianity is on its way out and is gradually disappearing. It is true that, in the longer term, we do not know the future of Christianity here in Western Europe. And it is true that in some places there is indeed little ecclesiastical presence. But to conclude from this that the Church or Christianity are indeed disappearing is a gratuitous claim. There are too many signs of renewal and vitality that disprove such a statement. Crisis can also be a *kairos*, an opportunity. The situation and conditions in which the

Church can fulfill its mission are no longer those on which it could count for centuries, at least here in the West. The Church must leave a certain past behind and is on its way to a new future. But that future is still largely unknown. Hence, the feeling of uncertainty, the feeling of crisis. But nothing shows that there will be no future!

Some point an accusing finger at the Second Vatican Council, saying that it is the changes and innovations of this Council that have brought the Church into uncertainty and crisis. If not so much had changed back then, it is asserted, then everything would have remained the same. That is, of course, putting the cart before the horse. That our society has changed so fundamentally is truly not the result of decisions of this Council. The Council did not change the situation. The Council was convened precisely because the situation had fundamentally changed. Like it or not, a radical transformation within Western culture has simultaneously and inevitably changed the situation of the Church within that culture. It is in this changed situation that the Church must fulfill its mission. It is, by the way, the Council that has helped us and still helps us to be able to turn the page and discern what the Church's place is within that society and what place it deserves.

2

A Religious and Secular Society

BEFORE CONTINUING our reflection, we should first clarify the necessary concepts. What is meant by a religious culture and a religious society? And what is the secular character of the society that is ours today?

Culture is the way in which a person inhabits his or her world. The human person would not survive in the wild. Not only does he or she have to work the earth but he or she must also build his or her world by oneself. Culture is nature as the human re-creates and expands it so that one can live and dwell there and share life with others. Culture is not only about the fine arts. It has a much broader meaning. Culture structures all the components and dimensions of human existence. In the course of their history and to this day, all people live on the same earth. But they don't all inhabit this earth in the same way. Hence, there is a plurality of cultures. Much depends on the options and the choices one makes in the development of one's world. Those choices and those options are not necessarily the same for everyone.

These options largely determine the individuality and identity of a culture or a civilization. Because there are, indeed, choices to be made! First, there is the distinction between what is true and what is not true. One cannot live in a world in which this distinction is not made. There can be no permanent living in the lie. The same applies to the distinction between good and evil. One cannot live in a world where moral indifference is the rule. Certainly, the same choices are not necessarily always made here. But it is inevitable to make choices. Not doing so means the end of civilization and the return to the law of the jungle.

It is not possible for one to situate and maintain oneself in a world where anything is permitted and where boundaries and taboos do not exist—a world where there is no consensus on what is or is not permissible. The distinction between what is allowed and what is not allowed is constitutive for every culture. Hence, we understand the importance of a body that regulates the relationships between people, maintains public order, and therefore, can also sanction. The rule of law and political order, therefore, belong to the very heart of every culture. And of course, art and artistic expression will also be specific to a certain culture.

These are the components of every culture: thought, morality, law, politics, and art. And of course, also, at least until the rise of modernity, religion. Indeed, until the rise of modernity, because before that all cultures were religious cultures. In religious cultures, religion plays a decisive role. Religion is not only one of the components of culture; it is ultimately the determining factor within that culture.

People's thoughts: what they hold to be true or false; their moral views: what is allowed and what is not allowed; the law and the way in which human relations are regulated, political decision-making, art, everything is permeated by religious thought. That is not to say that in such societies everyone is an actively engaged and convinced believer. But religion is the frame of reference, the "worldview," in which people think and act.

It is in this sense that Christianity has been the cultural religion in the West for centuries. These Christian roots are undeniable. Christianity had already integrated the great Greco-Latin culture of antiquity. Christianity has not only been one of the components of Western civilization, it was the soul of it. It is from biblical and Christian thought that Western civilization formed after antiquity. For centuries, Western culture has been a Christian culture. Christianity was a "cultural religion." It was from there, by the way, that the rise of modernity was also possible.

What, then, is the secular character of a culture? A secular culture does not necessarily mean a culture where religion is absent. Religion may even be one of the components of that culture. But religion is not the body that determines the other components. In a religious culture, there is one cultural religion. In a secular culture, there can be different religions and beliefs. Religious belief is a matter of a free and personal choice of the citizen. But society itself is not a religious society. There is nothing to prevent believers or Christians from being present in that society. But Christianity no longer has the status of "cultural religion." It is no longer the frame of reference of the culture.

It is not because Christianity no longer has this status that it is therefore on its way out or in decline, even though there are those who think so. They see that the number of Christians is decreasing along with the influence of the Church and its beliefs in society. They conclude from this that the Christian faith is gradually disappearing and that a secular culture ultimately means the end of Christianity. This is still a somewhat peculiar conclusion. One really cannot be surprised that the number of believers and Christians here in the West has decreased. The opposite would be truly surprising and even incomprehensible.

It is true that we do not know the future of Christianity in our regions, at least not in the long term. But the fact that the Western world has become secular, and Christianity no longer occupies the central place in it, in no way means that it is therefore disappearing. It can also be present in that culture in a different way. In Asia and Africa, for example, Christianity has never had that position. But it is present and not without vitality. Here in the West, it has had that position for centuries, as Islam still has in many Muslim countries. There is nothing to suggest that the future of Christianity necessarily depends on its status as a cultural religion.

The question of whether this would be the case for Islam here in the West is open. There are neither compelling nor sufficient reasons for that to be the case. As far as Christianity is concerned, there is no hesitation: that status is by no means assumed. It is not true that Christianity can only develop and maintain itself if it can indeed acquire that status. Christianity does not assume that the world in which it accomplishes its mission must itself be Christian. Where this is the case, it is rather the exception.

3

The Emergence of a Christian Culture

HOW IS IT THAT, since antiquity and for such a long period of time, Christianity has been the cultural religion here in the West? What made that possible? And how is it that it started to lose that position? An answer to these questions is necessary to understand our contemporary situation and our times.

Let us not forget that in the West, Christianity was originally a foreign religion. The names of the days that are still in use testify to this. They refer to ancient ancestral gods. Our forefathers were not Christians. Christianity originated in the Middle East and has grown up within the culture of late antiquity. It is in the third and fourth centuries that Christianity formed itself in terms of content and became socially and culturally profiled.[1] This was possible because it continued the Jewish mono-theistic tradition but integrated with Greco-Latin culture. The Church fathers belonged intellectually and culturally to the avant-garde of their time.

Additionally, in late antiquity the traditional religiosity was no longer popular with many. Many people had a great regard for the Jewish monothe-istic faith. Few people realize how much Judaism was spread throughout the civilized world around the Mediterranean at that time. This can be seen, for example, in Paul's travels: to whatever city he travels, he goes to the synagogue. And it is there that he, as a Jew, could also take the floor. Juda-ism had really spread widely. Not a few people felt attracted by the Jewish faith and by monotheism. They did not become Jews. They are called "God-fearing" in the New Testament. They were people who did not allow themselves to be circumcised, but who adhered to Jewish belief. The earliest Christianity and the early missionary activity of the Church can be understood as an extension of this phenomenon.

---

1. See Marie-Françoise Baslez, *Comment les chrétiens sont devenus catholiques: 1er–5e siècle* (Paris: Éditions Tallandier, 2019).

Of course, Christianity is not just an extension of Judaism. It has its own identity and originality. It is precisely this individuality that determined its future. It has been successful in ancient times precisely because it made a difference. But it remains true that the individuality of Christianity can only be understood in its enduring connection with the Jewish faith. The Christian faith understands itself as the fulfillment of the Scriptures. But they are indeed the same Scriptures. As Jesus puts it in the parable of the rich man and Lazarus, "If they do not listen to Moses and the prophets, neither will they be convinced even if someone rises from the dead" (Luke 16:31). The Church cannot understand its own faith and mission apart from its link with the Jewish people. For the Christian, Judaism is not simply one of the other religions. Christianity and Judaism are too intimately connected for that. Both are situated within the same biblical tradition.

To understand the growth of Christianity during late antiquity, it is important to realize the profound difference between the deity of which biblical tradition testifies and the gods who were worshiped everywhere. The deity of which Scripture testifies is a God who enters into relationship with humanity. That makes God unique. Because the other gods don't. Of course, there is also a relationship between the deity and the people there. They follow the necessary cult. For them, however, these divine powers—personifications of natural and cosmic forces—are unpredictable and arbitrary. They can always turn against humans. They therefore need to be acknowledged.

But those gods are not really interested in humans. They are also not interested in what people do to each other. Whether people pursue the good or not is none of their business. And as far as relationships are concerned, those gods are only interested in each other. They are gods who are concerned only with themselves, with their own glory. "Paganism did not deny any friendship between the deity and the chosen individual...but it had no sense of any passionate and mutual relationship of love and authority, a relationship that never ends, but is not occasional as in paganism, for it is as essential to God as it is to the human."[2] Irenaeus, who was bishop in Lyon in the second century, could not have better expressed the individuality of the biblical God than when he said, *Gloria Dei vivens homo; vita autem hominis visio Dei*— the glory of God is the life of the human; and the

---

2. Paul Veyne, *Quand notre monde est devenu chrétien (312-394)* (Paris: Albin Michel, 2007), 43.

human's life is that he or she may see God. In it, God has set his honor and glory: that humans may live, a human life worthy of that name, and that they may find that life in their encounter and communion with God.

The biblical God is unique in every sense of the word: not just because the biblical God the only God but also because this God is not like the other gods. Unique not only in the numerical sense of the word, but also because the biblical God is a stranger in the pantheon of the gods. For the biblical God is a God who relates to humanity and is not indifferent. What people do and experience, God cares about. It concerns a God who stands in solidarity and is connected to the fate of creation and of humanity. That is precisely why God wants to be known. God longs to be known and loved by men and women. That is precisely why God created humans. Creation is already focused on the Covenant. God did not create just to scatter people! If God calls or creates others to life, it is precisely because God wants to share life and love.

Psalm 51 is so eloquent in that sense. The Psalmist prays to God,

> For you have no delight in sacrifice....
> The sacrifice acceptable to God is a

> broken spirit;
> a broken and contrite heart, O God,
>   you will not despise. (Ps 51:16–17)

Those few words lead us to the heart of biblical faith. Not that the cult no longer makes sense. No matter how critical the prophets of Israel have often been of cult practice, they have never denied the right of the cult, but only that the sacrifices only make sense within the relationship of trust and love between God and humans. In Psalm 82, God addresses the other gods and says,

> How long will you judge unjustly
>   and show partiality to the wicked?
> Give justice to the weak and the orphan;
>   maintain the right of the lowly and
>   the destitute.
> Rescue the weak and the needy;
>   deliver them from the hand of the
>   wicked. (Ps 82:2–4)

Impressive is what Psalm 145 says about God:

> The LORD is gracious and merciful,
>   slow to anger and abounding in
>   steadfast love.
> The LORD is good to all,

and his compassion is over all that he
has made. (Ps 145:8–9)

This relationship between God and human-
ity, here, is really a relationship of love. The central words in the Book of Deuteronomy testify to
it. They contain the creed of Israel and at the same
time express the first and great commandment:
"Hear, O Israel, the LORD is our God, the LORD alone.
You shall love the LORD your God with all your
heart, and with all your soul, and with all your
might" (Deut 6:4). Only two verbs are used here:
"hear" and "love." They are the key words for any
true relationship. Already in Jewish tradition, the
link is made with the other commandment in the
Book of Leviticus: "You shall love your neighbor
as yourself" (Lev 19:18). In the Gospel of Luke, it
is the scribe who, in response to Jesus's question,
connects the two commandments. Jesus only has
his answer to confirm.

Yet the order cannot be reversed: love of God
contains the first commandment. But the second
is like the first (Matt 22:39) and therefore equally
necessary. They cannot be separated. One cannot happen without the other. As it says later in
John's first letter,

> Those who say "I love God" and hate
> their brothers or sisters are liars; for
> those who do not love a brother or sister
> whom they have seen, cannot love God
> whom they have not seen. (1 John 4:20)

As Paul will say in Romans, "Love is the fulfilling of the law" (Rom 13:10).

All this must be borne in mind if one is to
understand the presence of early Christianity in
late antiquity. Christianity is rooted in this biblical tradition. Of course, it also has its irreducible
individuality. But it is about the same God, the God
of the covenant. A God who is not smug enough
just being God, who wants to meet and share. This
is how Israel has become God's people, the people
who belong to God. The message of the New Testament radicalizes this belief: God not only wanted
to share life with us; God didn't just want to con-
nect with us and tie together our fates. "When the
fullness of time had come" (Gal 4:4), God shared
our human existence. In everything to us equal
"except in sin." God has shared our finiteness and
fragility. It is the mystery of the incarnation of
God that, however original, can only be correctly
understood from the biblical faith of God seeking
humankind. That was the new sound: God's love is

so great that God wanted to be not only with us, but also like us. One can no longer imagine what new sound the gospel made for the society of that time.

It is only after antiquity that Christianity finally established itself here in the West. In that late antiquity, Christianity was present here in our regions only in a few places and in a few important centers. I am thinking of Trier, once the residence of the Western Roman emperor, but also about Tongeren, Tournai, and Cambrai. They are also the oldest bishop's seats. Consider the cultural chaos the West found itself in after the fall of the Roman Empire. It is also the moment when other peoples and tribes invaded and settled here: the Lombards, the Goths, and especially the Franks. It is only through the evangelization of the sixth and seventh centuries that Christianity finally established itself in these places.

Already during the last two centuries of antiquity, Christianity had become indispensable both religiously and culturally. The Church had succeeded in fully integrating itself into the culture and society of the time. Initially, there was hesitation: Was not the field of action aimed at Judaism? Was the gospel to be brought to other peoples and nations? We know how tearing that question was for early Christianity. But it was also so decisive for the future of the Church. Paul played a crucial role in this. He helped the Church discern the path it needed to take so as to be faithful to its mission.

In this way, the Church has gradually been able to grow, not separately or alongside the society in which it lived, but precisely by participating in it and integrating itself into it. It is in that world and addressing that society that it has proclaimed the gospel of Christ and of God's love, partly in response to the great questions and challenges of the people of that time. The Church managed to touch the hearts of ancient people. The Church showed that it was part of that culture, right down to the way it expressed its faith. At the fall of the Western Roman Empire, when the culture of antiquity collapsed here completely, it was the Church that had partly absorbed this culture. It was therefore the only body that could preserve and pass on the remains of this great culture. It was the only body on which the new political rulers could rely to rebuild society. The baptism of Clovis demonstrates this fully.

The result should not be so surprising: in a long and complex process, a Christian civilization gradually developed. Theoretically, of course, this could also have evolved into a situation in which no religion took on the function of cultural religion, neither Christianity nor any of the ancestral religions. In fact, that possibility did not exist. Before the rise of modernity, cultures were always religious cultures. That is precisely the peculiarity of modern secular culture: no religion determines the culture as such. If after antiquity one of the existing religions had to be chosen, the choice had already been made. Christianity was the only eligible religion.

Did the desire for influence and power on the part of the Church also play a role in this? For it is true, the cultural status gives the religion in question an extremely influential and determining position, and therefore, also power. Can the development of the Church after antiquity be understood in this sense? I think this interpretation looks at the past mainly from the perspective of the presuppositions and the horizon of understanding modernity. Of course, power has played a role. Wherever a religion becomes a cultural religion or even a state religion, the risks of derailment and abuse of power are far from imaginary. But I think I do justice to history when it is stated that the historical circumstances have forced this cultural position of Christianity. For the Church, it was also a matter of responsibility. It is only after, and thanks to modernity, that we can distinguish between the mission of the Church as a cultural religion and its actual mission as a Church, called and sent to proclaim the gospel and to be a sign of God's love in the midst of society.

Thus, after antiquity, Christianity gradually became the cultural religion of the West. Culture and faith form one whole. Society had become a Christian society. Of course, all this did not happen in one day, but it took several centuries. It is from the tenth century that one can say that the West is Christian. Everything was penetrated by the Christian faith and Christian ideas. And as is the case for all religious cultures, this encompasses all aspects of culture: thought and philosophy, morality, law, politics, and art. Faith became socially self-evident. One lived in a Christian world. Of course, there were always dissident currents. We even find them in medieval society. Just think of the Cathars and everything that has been done to eradicate them. There was, of course, Islam: the "Turk," as the Muslim was called in the Middle Ages.

But Islam was beyond the boundaries of Christendom. And there were also the Jews. Judaism, older than Christianity and already present in antiquity, was the only exception tolerated within Christendom, more or less, because the situation of the Jews was always very precarious, with all the consequences that entails. One knows what happened in 1492 after the *Reconquista* when Jews were expelled from Spain. Again and again, discriminatory measures or the pogrom threatened. After the coming of Christ, one could no longer imagine the existence and presence of Judaism. Paul had said of the Christians coming out of paganism that they had been "cut from what is by nature a wild olive tree and grafted, contrary to nature, into a cultivated olive tree" (Rom 11:24). Yet for the Church, Judaism no longer had a right to exist alongside it. According to the thinking of the time, the Church had replaced Judaism. Yet this theory of substitution was by no means determined by the Christian faith itself. It was mainly its role as a cultural religion that was responsible for it. A cultural religion does not tolerate other religious traditions besides it. This shows how dangerous religious cultures can be. Dangerous especially for minorities. How greatly the most recent Vatican Council has opened our eyes to this reality.

4

The Rise of Modernity

THE RISE OF MODERN culture marked the end of the monopoly that Christianity had as a cultural religion. Just as the Christianization had required several centuries, so too did the evolution to a modern and secular civilization. It was a complex and lengthy process.

The Reformation in the sixteenth century was an important factor in this evolution—not that there is a direct link between the Reformation and the Enlightenment. Martin Luther had no intention of founding another church. He wanted to reform the Church but did not succeed in this. Eventually, Christianity itself became divided and was split into several Christian confessions. It is this decomposition of Christianity that, among other factors, enabled the emergence of another culture. Instead of the one Church, there was now a multitude of churches and confessions. Christianity itself was now in the plural. One wasn't just a Christian anymore. One was Catholic, Lutheran, or Reformed.

By pluralizing Christianity, the Reformation also put it into perspective. However, the reform itself did not draw this conclusion. Each confession continued to absolutize its own viewpoint. Could one of those Christian confessions adopt the status of cultural religion? Could Christianity remain a cultural religion in the long run? After long consultations and especially after long years of war and violence, they finally had to answer no to that question.

Let us not forget that the Reformation did not lead to the reformation of the Church. It actually brought division, a division that led to the wars of religion throughout Europe and even into the newly discovered overseas territories. If the Reformation changed the relativization of Christianity, then the religious wars radically extended it. Initially, it was thought that the matter could be arranged by country or region. Already at the

Peace of Augsburg in 1555, Charles V had accepted this situation for the German territories and principalities of the Holy Roman Empire. If in a certain country or region the monarch was Catholic or Lutheran, let his subjects also be Catholic or Lutheran: *Cuius regio illius et religio.* A convenient solution. But of course, it doesn't work that way. Will a subject in matters of faith just follow his prince? And what if the monarch changes confession, which effectively happened sometimes? So, the wars continued.

After a short period of peace, violence and wars flared up again in all their intensity from 1618 onward—for thirty years, until 1648. It is not without reason that this Thirty Years' War can be called a First World War.[1] And, of course, it wasn't just about religious matters. More and more, the *raison d'Etat* took precedence. Cardinal de Richelieu's foreign policy in France is the telling example of this. The devastation was enormous and had to stop. From 1646, all representatives of the states and principalities met in Osnabrück and Münster for the peace talks. On October 24, 1648, the Peace of Westphalia was signed in Münster. It

---

1. Dick Harrison, *De Dertigjarige Oorlog. De allereerste wereldoorlog 1618-1648* (Utrecht: Omniboek, 2018).

is one of the most important dates to understand the rise of modern culture.

When asked whether one of the confessions could be permanently recognized as a cultural religion, the answer in Münster was of course negative. It would only continue the wars. Even though religion remained a state matter for a long time, it became clear that, regarding the choice of a religious belief, one could not simply follow the monarch. It was gradually becoming a matter of personal and free choice. If violence and war were to be avoided, tolerance was the only way. The Treaty of Münster[2] was not just a step forward. It was a break with the past. Especially since it made the next inevitable step: it is not up to the monarch to determine the religion for his subjects. That choice belongs to the individual citizen. Everyone chooses the religion or confession he or she wants. A page had been turned. Times had changed. It represented a definitive step toward modernity.

No wonder freedom was written at the heart of the emerging new culture. This was not just about some changes, however important, within Western culture. It was indeed about the change

---

2. Treaty of Münster refers to two treaties signed in 1648 and forms part of the Peace of Westphalia ending the Thirty Years' War.

of the culture itself and therefore the emergence of a new culture. People no longer lived in a world where only one of the Christian confessions was in charge. And what had become true for the various Christian denominations would gradually also apply to the different religions. It was not only about the legitimacy of the various Christian churches, but gradually about the legitimacy of religious pluralism, and finally—after a long road—the right not to have a religious position.

When the importance of the wars of religion is emphasized here to understand the beginnings of modern culture, it obviously does not exclude other factors. These are also as decisive as the Reformation and the wars that followed. One thinks here of the Renaissance and of the rediscovery of antiquity, precisely in its pre-Christian status. In it came the realization that great civilizations could exist even without Christianity. The great impetus of cultural change also came, of course, from the development of the sciences and especially the positive sciences. For it was precisely because of this that the freedom and emancipation of the human person became a real possibility. After all, what is the significance of freedom and emancipation if the means to realize them are lacking? It is the sciences that would make these possible and that would so strongly determine people's perceptions. And in all of this, the eighteenth century, the century of the Enlightenment, has been the catalyst.

Thus, there is more than one factor and more than one circumstance that has prepared and enabled a culture based on freedom and emancipation. Freedom and emancipation would indeed become the great values of this new culture. It would no longer be around faith in God and the human's final destiny that culture and society would be built, but around the values of freedom, emancipation, and progress. It was also no longer one or the other religion that would determine the culture and hold it together. For Luther and his contemporaries, the crucial and existential question had been whether God was merciful to people and thus whether they could escape the final judgment. Now, all attention is focused on the human self—one takes one's own destiny into one's own hands.

What will henceforth combine all forces is no longer faith in God but in the human self and human possibilities. The gaze will no longer be fixed on heaven but on the world, the *saeculum* for which the human person knows oneself responsible and for which the development of the sciences will provide the person with the means to make that world habitable. It has been a long process, a long and complex evolution that, in truth, has meant a revolution. Only afterward does it become clear that this is about a different view of reality, a different understanding of being human, a different way of situating oneself in the world and before others. In other words, another culture, another world.

This shift in culture and society inevitably raised the question not only of the place of Christianity and of the Church, but also of religion as such. It is the end of a Christian world. The end of a religious culture.

5

What Do We Have to Do?

OW TO RESPOND to this situation? Trying to turn the tide? Or fully adapt? How can the Church position itself in such a situation? These are questions that are raised in many church debates. It is, by the way, the question with which Islam is inevitably confronted here in the West.

First, it is important and necessary for the Church to accept this changed situation. The Church must subscribe to the legitimacy of a secular culture. It can no longer position itself as a cultural religion. This does not mean that it has to adapt and conform to everything that has become common and self-evident in that culture. It's like the situation of a migrant. One cannot be asked to deny one's own identity and tradition. One is not asked to assimilate. But one must integrate oneself into the society that receives him or her. Because it is within that society that from now on one will share life with the other citizens to build a society together with them. One has no right to impose one's tradition on the whole of society.

Here I think of the beautiful Letter to Diognetus dating from the second or early third century. It describes very well the situation of Christians in the society at that time, and how they were then integrated into society without losing their individuality, completely in the world and yet not of the world:

> Christians are distinguished from other people neither by their place of residence nor by language nor by customs. After all, nowhere do they live in their own cities, nor do they speak a separate dialect or lead a special life....They live in the cities of the Greeks and other peoples, as fate has it for each, and they follow the customs of their land in clothing and food and in their further necessities of life. They live their lives in a way

that arouses admiration and, according to general judgment, appears as something incredible. They live in their own homeland, but as if they were foreigners established there. They have everything in common with the others as citizens, and they have to endure all sorts of things as strangers. Every foreign country is their homeland and every homeland is their foreign land. Like everyone else, they marry and produce children. But they do not kill unborn life. Their table is common, but not their bed. They are in the flesh, but do not live according to the flesh.

So it is with the Church. It is called to fulfill and integrate into secular and pluralistic culture. It must not cling to an earlier stage of culture. But it does not mean that it has to adapt itself to all the elements of a secular culture, because modernity is also increasingly pushing its own limits today. It is no coincidence that postmodernity is spoken of. But it remains true that we no longer live in a Christian society. We really need to accept and internalize this personally and make our own. Not because we are obliged to do so, for it is in fact unavoidable, but wholeheartedly. If the Church wants to face its future with faith and trust, with daring and courage, it must accept this real situation as the place where God calls, knowing fully that the Church's faith and Christian convictions are no longer the cultural religion of society.

The end of Christendom in no way signifies is the end of Christianity, but the end of Christianity's social position. Christianity and the Church have been the determining factors in the construction of society here for centuries. They inevitably had an extremely influential position. But nowhere in the New Testament does it say that this is their ideal position, nor that that position is most peculiar to them. Hence, the central questions for the future: Can Christianity be vital even without this position? Can we also be Christians and Church in a non-Christian world?

That is the question that Islam is also facing today: Can Islam be situated within a Western, European, non-Islamic culture? Christianity has struggled with this question in recent centuries and—it must be acknowledged—has resisted the rise of modern culture very strongly in the beginning and for longer than necessary. It has been a difficult and painful road for the Church. The Second Vatican Council played a crucial role in the acceptance process. It means the Church's official yes to modern culture as a context in which it can fulfill her mission.

Indeed, the Second Vatican Council opened the way to finding answers to challenges in such a changed time. These are questions relating to the Church herself: what it deeply belongs to and what it is called to do by God, the Church's speaking about God and God's revelation, the Church's liturgy, and its structure of authority. But there is also the question of how the Church situates herself in society and how it strives for a more humane and just society based on faith. And of course, there is the question of how the Church relates to those who do not belong to its full community and to those who do not share its faith.

What the Council said about the relationship with the other Christian churches and communities, about the relationship with the other religions, and not in the least about religious freedom, has opened doors that until now remained largely closed. It is far from an exaggeration to call this Council truly providential. Without this Council, the Church today would have reached a complete impasse, locked in itself and in its own discourse, and powerless in the face of the challenges of our time.

Let me provide a small example to clarify what I mean by accepting the situation. It is constantly heard in the media and in public opinion that the churches are emptying. Unspoken, it is said that the Church is not doing well, and that faith and Church are gradually regressing. It is constantly suggested that many are leaving the Church. I would answer that they are not leaving the Church, but rather they have never entered it. Above all, the churches cannot all be full. There are full churches today and churches that are well attended, but not all of them. The infrastructure of the number of churches is designed for a situation in which everyone or most of the population went to church. It is designed for the situation under Christendom and no longer corresponds to the real situation of the Church in our society.

The thesis of the continuous emptying of the churches (so they should have been empty by now!) is still based on the assumption that everyone should go to church. It is striking how in the subconscious Christianity is still thought of as a cultural religion. But that is precisely the question. Of course, the gospel must be proclaimed to all and all are invited to celebrate the liturgy. But in society as it has become today, it is evident that not everyone is Christian or religious. It is not the inhabitants of a village or a hamlet who gather on Sunday for the Eucharist, but the Christians. Of course, not all who call themselves Christians will be present every Sunday. But this is not to say that they are therefore quietly dropping out. There are different degrees of belonging to the Church. However, the fact that there are churches that are not visited much anymore or no longer, does not mean that the Christian faith in our society is disappearing. That is not an omen of the end of Christianity. It is the inevitable consequence of a change within our culture and society. We live in a secular and pluralistic society. That explains why not all churches are full and cannot be. Furthermore, this reality shows how important it is to analyze and understand the situation properly.

6

Modernity and Its Limits

THE QUESTIONS REMAIN: Can Christianity hold its own and does the Church have a future in a world that has become secular and is therefore no longer Christian? My response to these questions has so far been positive. Nevertheless, this will have to be argued further. There is at least one argument of great importance: the issue of religious freedom and of the freedom of the act of faith. We have already shown how much religious freedom is threatened in religious cultures. Cultures defined and shaped by one specific religion hardly tolerate other beliefs or options. Minorities are always under threat.

In religious cultures, faith is an option of the culture itself and not primarily a personal choice. Of course, in such a situation, people can also make faith a personal choice. The facts would be wronged by stating that, for example, in medieval culture people were Christians merely because of a sociological law. But it is true that in such a situation the personal faith of a person is also carried by the whole society and the prevailing culture. There is no real freedom of choice. That is the case in a modern secular society. Here, the Christian faith is no longer the option of culture itself. It is the personal option of the citizen who is free to adhere to this or that belief, free to believe or not to believe. For modernity, that freedom is generally supported. We'll return to that later. But freedom is equally precious to the Christian faith. There is no faith without freedom, at least no faith that deserves that name. For faith is the free response of a person to God who makes God-self known to him or her and wants to enter into a relationship.

In our modern culture, this freedom of faith regains its full significance. On this point, modernity and Christian faith are not contradictory. In this sense, our culture is truly an opportunity for the believer to rediscover that freedom and to reconnect with the heart of our faith. For faith, in its deepest essence, is not the acceptance of a doctrine or an idea, but the personal encounter with God. Let us not be blind to what is happening more and more today: that many of our contemporaries are looking for something that can give meaning and support to their lives and that there are also among them those who are rediscovering the expressiveness and beauty of the Christian faith.

Yet there are voices that say that in the long run modern and secular culture means the end, not only of Christianity but of religion as such. They say that freedom and emancipation will eventually lead to emancipation from any religious bond, that autonomy and self-determination does not tolerate any body outside of itself. If this is so, it does indeed mean the end of the belief in God. That is the thesis of dogmatic secularism, blind and without awareness of the actual limits of modernity. It is a radicalization of secularization. Just like a religious belief, a secular belief can also radicalize. In a modern culture, the demand for God will not disappear. Neither does its social relevance. Modernity cannot absolutize itself without crossing its own boundaries, and without endangering society itself. It is precisely the limitation that shows that the question of God will always be asked again and will never be silenced. The question of God will inevitably remain a pertinent question for humankind itself and for the coexistence of people. Let me explain.

Modern culture offers us the framework in which we can live together, in respect and with respect for each other's freedom and diversity. If freedom is one of the fundamental human rights of every human being and of every citizen, then this right also applies to my fellow human and fellow citizen who is different from me. In a modern society, the government guarantees the freedom of every citizen and of every minority. The rule of law exists precisely to protect the minority and to guarantee freedom. Everyone needs to abide by these rules. It is not the religious laws that govern society, nor the torah, nor the gospel, nor sharia. In this sense, modern culture contains fundamental values that, in our diversity, we nevertheless jointly pursue and respect. They make up the right and legitimacy of a modern secular society that we want to defend against all forms of exclusion and extremism, and against any religion or ideology that wants to impose itself on the whole of society.

Nevertheless, legitimate and necessary as this secular culture is, it is not the body that gives meaning to life nor to our commitment to society. Otherwise, it would become precisely the ideology that wants to impose itself on the whole of society. It is not itself a worldview. Secular culture cannot give meaning and direction to the life of a person, to his or her actions, nor can it present itself as the *pensée unique* for the whole of society. It cannot replace religion as a kind of civil religion. If modernity wants to remain true to its origins and to its legitimacy, it must accept that limit. What religion has done and sometimes still does, as a cultural religion, it cannot do. That is precisely why modernity came into being. It cannot define and structure the entire culture. This culture is essentially pluralistic. Modernity must be the first to respect and guarantee that pluralism and the freedom of the citizen and of every human person.

It is precisely regarding the question of the meaning and purpose of human freedom that modern secular culture reaches its limits. Freedom is a great good and a fundamental human right. It is the greatness of modern culture to guarantee it. But when it comes to the question of the meaning of my freedom, that culture leaves me hungry. It tells me that I am free. But it doesn't tell me what to do. On that question, it always throws the ball back: do what you want. But that's not an answer. Because what do I want? Surely, it can't be about the first accidental desire that comes to mind. There are impulses, drives, and desires in me that I don't want.

This is not just a question of what is or is not morally justifiable. It's not just an ethical issue—a question of whether I should do this or not—it's an existential question of meaning. In other words, it's about what I do with my life. Because I can also lose my life in banality and meaninglessness. How do I live and how do I commit myself so that my life is worth living? I am free, but to do what? And for whom? These are questions that not only the believer asks oneself but inevitable questions for every human being.

A secular culture does not answer these questions. The only thing it tells me—and it is not insignificant—is that I can answer the question in complete freedom and that no one has the right to impose any answer on others. Of itself, that culture only tells me that I must take my destiny into my own hands to fully experience my freedom and give it every chance. I am quite free...to be as free as possible. Self-development, emancipation, and progress: they are the very goals of modern culture. It is its greatness but at the same time its limit.

It is as though progress itself is the meaning of my existence and of my actions. Everything happens in the name of progress. Good is what progress serves. That sound is also heard in bioethical issues. Any extension of the euthanasia law is seen as a "progressive" measure, a sign of progress. Progress in what way? In what kind of society? How does a person feel about oneself? What kind of society do we want? What is society if progress itself is the meaning of everything we practice? Of course, this concept is well suited when it comes to scientific, technical, or economic progress. Indeed, medical science can be said to have made spectacular progress. But surely it is difficult to apply the concept of progress to other areas and sectors of life. For example, there is no mention of progress in the world of art, is there? In the end, what is true emancipation and progress? Are they always a step forward in the history of human civilization? As Pope Paul VI put it, real progress must be integral and thus relate not only to every human being but also to the whole of humanity: "Development cannot be reduced merely to economic growth. To be real, it must be complete, that is, promote every person and the whole person."[1]

---

1. Pope Paul VI, *Populorum Progressio*, no. 14.

This also applies to freedom and emancipation. What is freedom? It can't just be about the ability to do what I want, can it? Surely, it cannot be just about my individual self-development? I share life with others. My freedom is specific. It is not absolute. I don't always do what I want. Thank goodness! Freedom also involves availability. There is no freedom without fraternity. What would be the point of a freedom that always simply makes me fold back on myself and does not make me available to others? Why else would I commit myself to something or someone without benefiting myself, sometimes quite the contrary? Why can parents go so far in loving their severely disabled child? Why care about the fate of the poor? Why worry about the fate of refugees? Why do I commit myself to a more humane and fraternal society? Why do I feel responsible for future generations and commit myself to the environment and the preservation of creation? Why do I feel responsible? It is Cain's question: "Am I my brother's keeper?" (Gen 4:9).

It is what threatens our culture and the future of our society: an individualistic view of life and the globalization of indifference. Why commit myself to something that will not bring me any benefit, that will limit my freedom and will not help me in any way to shape my self-development? To the question of what I should do, for what or for whom I am committed, and therefore, the question of the meaning of my freedom and my actions, there are no rational or scientific answers. Yet, we know from experience that it is what gives meaning to our lives and guarantees a humane society. There are choices and commitments about which modern culture itself neither inspires nor motivates. But choices and commitments enable our society to do what it is called to do: to be a humane society. Many seek and find the meaning of their lives and the meaning of their life choices precisely in their religious beliefs. That is why religious beliefs have such a clear and invaluable social significance. Of course, there is a separation of Church and state. But there is no separation between faith and society. If I am a citizen in society, then I also do it as a Christian. Or rather, it is my faith that helps me discover my true citizenship. In civil society, the Christian is a loyal citizen.

Our question does not focus on modernity as such. Yet the question is whether a secularist culture and mentality does not stand in the way of the true progress and development of the human: precisely in what makes us human. Is such a culture truly sustainable? The human is a deeply religious being, marked by the desire for the Absolute. I am not saying a Christian, but a meaning-seeking and in that sense also a religious being. Of course, that doesn't mean that everyone will be a believer or religious. Religious belief is a personal option that is taken in freedom. But to say that religion is henceforth a purely optional phenomenon, meaningful only for the private life of the citizen, without further social or cultural relevance, is a belief that, rationally, is not very compelling. Religion is a universal human phenomenon. We are the first to say that it is not constitutive for humankind, but an option for some who are interested in it in their personal lives.

7

The Privatization of Religion

THE SEPARATION OF church and state can no longer be called into question. It is an essential achievement of modernity. Before the rise of modernity, this was only possible in part precisely because Christianity had become the cultural religion here in the West. One could not think of Church and Christianity as distinct from all social and political life, with all the tensions and conflicts that entailed. This goes without saying for all religious cultures: all cultural, social, and political life was imbued with Christian thought.

I have already referred to those who believe that modern secular culture means, in the long run, the end of all religious belief. Faith and modernity would ultimately be mutually exclusive. It is, in my view, an expression of dogmatic secularism. Not everyone, however, is so extreme in the current debate about religion and society. In addition to this extreme view, today there is also another point of view that is widespread and perhaps more extensive. This point of view has no problem with someone being religious. After all, everyone is free to think what he or she wants. Faith belongs to free speech. But religious beliefs, it is claimed, have no social relevance. They can have significance for citizens' private lives, but not for society as such. According to this viewpoint, they have no social significance and should not interfere in social and public debate.

The proposition of the privatization of religion touches the heart and meaning of Christian faith and of religious belief. For the believer, there is really no separation between faith and life, just as there is no separation between faith and living together. We have just shown that there are questions to which a secular culture alone does not provide an answer. Questions one doesn't even ask. They are questions about the meaning of our existence and everything for which or for whom we are committed. It is those choices and those commitments that determine the meaning of our lives and our coexistence. I already made it clear: those choices and commitments, however personal, are of the highest social relevance. That is the fundamental reason why the privatization of religion is not a good thing. As far as Christianity is concerned, it is all too clear: the gospel not only relates to my private life, but it also motivates me in my social actions. It tells me where God wants to go with this world. It tells me what truly human life is and what is real progress.

It is not claimed here that religions would be the only source of meaning and motivation. Of course, even those who are not religious or have a nonreligious belief can give meaning to their actions and commit themselves to a more human and just society. Religions do not have a monopoly on this. But they are themselves a source of hope and meaning. Of course, it can also be the other way around. Religions can also be misused. Then they become a source of hatred and violence or become an opium through which people become alienated from themselves and from reality. Anything human can indeed be abused. But that's abuse. Religions are not like that by themselves. Not Islam. Not Christianity.

The gospel proclaimed by the Church is the good news of God's humanity. The call to humanity belongs essentially to Christianity and to the entire biblical faith tradition. And that is not just in theory. Surely one must be blind not to see how the gospel is a source of humanity in the true sense of the word. It engages us in our personal, family, and professional lives. But it also has a social impact. We don't just live each for himself or herself. The human is a social being, called to solidarity. And the gospel does not relate solely to the religious dimension of our existence. Perhaps some would like to have it like this: that the Church deals only with "religious" affairs. But the Church is not a world besides the actual world in which we live. It is in that world and sharing in all its challenges that it fulfills its mission.

The Church has no political power, but it is part of civil society. Nor does it mean that it wants nothing to do with the great challenges of society and of humanity. The Church does not live outside the world, nor above it, nor beside it. It is in the world that the Church lives and works and strives for a more just and humane world, together with the other religions and with all people of goodwill. What applies to the Church also applies to the Christian. A Christian who is socially committed does this not only as a citizen but also as a Christian. It is precisely faith that drives him or her to exercise responsible citizenship. The proposition of the privatization of religion does not do justice to the way believers experience their faith. Society and its government have every interest in respecting religions and valorizing their presence and commitment. It is there and in their initiatives that many find the strength and motivation to commit themselves to the common good.

It is therefore not good to undervalue or marginalize religions, because that is what we do when we reduce them to just our private life. It is like the secularist tendency within modern culture that is based on the now-dated idea that a world without religions is the best guarantee of emancipation and progress. After what happened in the twentieth century in Germany under the Nazi regime and in Russia and China under Marxist regimes, one should know better today.

But there is another reason why people today want to privatize religions as much as possible. That reason has to do with the growing presence of Islam here in the secular West. Want it or not, that presence has put religion back on the map.

However much one believes that religions can only be of some importance in private life, the presence of Islam is the subject of social debate. But not because Islam as a religion is considered so important. The reason is the danger of extremist and violent Islamism. Of course, that danger is real, and it would be irresponsible to deny it after so many Islamic terrorist attacks.

But it is equally irresponsible to identify Islam and Muslim believers with this extremism and this violence. As if Islam were violent in its capacity as a religion, then Christianity is equally so, because injustice and violence have indeed been committed in the name of the Christian faith over the course of history. Hinduism and even Buddhism cannot escape this reality either. It is all so true: like all that is human, religions can be misused, and no religion is immune to misuse. Religions are at risk, especially when they have the status of cultural religion. This has been the case for Christianity here in the West, and it is still the case for Islam in certain countries today.

But the possibility of misusing something does not mean that any use of it is out of the question. Injustice is being done to Islam and to the many Muslim believers here in the West by identifying them with terrorist violence. If we are right to want to combat terrorism and violence, then the privatization and marginalization of religion is not the appropriate method. It also shows little appreciation, neither for Islam nor for Christianity, which is then endorsed. If the privatization of religion, and Islam in particular, is the only response of a secular society to this development, then that is not only naive but, I fear, dangerous.

A few years ago, I was in Morocco with an official delegation of Jews, Christians, and Muslims. We visited some Jewish communities and, of course, especially high-ranking Muslim people. We also met the archbishop of Rabat. Needless to say, in this Muslim country there is also a small Christian community. He told us about the limited conditions under which the Church fulfills its mission there. The archbishop does not have Moroccan nationality, even though he was born there and will always be there. That is because he is a Christian. That's the way it is when a religion is a cultural religion. A Moroccan who asks for baptism is better off going abroad. The community that meets on Sundays consists of about six hundred Christians from the diplomatic or commercial world, but also especially young Africans, from below the Sahara, who come to study in Rabat.

The archbishop is president of the Organizing Authority for several Catholic schools. In these schools, of course, principals, teachers, and pupils are all Muslims, and no religious lessons are given. However, every year and for each of these schools he organizes a day of reflection for the management and teachers on the importance of their commitment to the education of young people. When asked what the meaning of these Catholic schools is, he replied that as Christians, we are also citizens of this country, and it is a way for us to contribute to the building up of a more humane and fraternal society.

Yet there remained a gnawing question: Why would one want to be present as Church in a country where pastoral opportunities are so limited? The archbishop's answer at the time touched me deeply. He replied, *"Pour montrer qu'il y a un autre chemin vers Dieu"* (To show that there is another way to God). He did not mean to show Muslims that we are right and that they are wrong. He spoke with the utmost respect about his country and about its Muslim believers. He just wanted to say that it is not good for the country if there is only one possibility in the religious field. That is neither good in Morocco nor elsewhere. He did not say it at all to defend the rights of the Church.

He expressed what secular modernity has taught us to see as a great good.

That is why it is unwise to privatize religion and, in this way, to marginalize and neutralize Christianity in particular. Not only because Christianity partly shares the roots of our civilization and permanently belongs to the historical and cultural heritage of the West. One does not despise one's own tradition. But mainly because this tendency toward privatization—especially if it continues generally and systematically—creates a void in the religious sphere that will be filled in any case. That is indeed what we need to be concerned about: that Islam would remain the only religious option left in a completely secularist culture.

It is an irreversible fact: Islam has established itself here in our Western society. Muslim believers are our fellow citizens. It's absurd to want to undo this. Our mission is to live together in the diversity of beliefs and to build a dignified and just society together. There is no other alternative. But that is precisely why it is so important that, in addition to Islam, there is and remains a vital Christianity, a living Church community, alongside the Jewish community and other beliefs and communities. It is also important that they promote peace and good relations among themselves, that they approach each other with reverence, without any proselytism, and that they meet and cherish interfaith dialogue as a precious commodity.

The danger is not Islam. The danger is that Islam would become the only religious option. This danger is precisely when the secularist mentality continues and religions, especially Christianity, are privatized and marginalized as much as possible. Islam as the only religious option would not be good. It is not good because it would prevent Islam from being located and integrated into the context of a secular culture and therefore into a culture in which Islam is not the cultural religion. Of course, it is not good for Christianity and the Church itself. But let us not forget that it would not be good for society either. The opposite would be harvested from what was sown. Secular society has every interest in appreciating and respecting religion and belief in their individuality.

PART II

WHY CHURCH?

In the first part of this book, I have tried to better understand the situation of the Church and of Christianity in today's Western culture. As a Church, we no longer live and engage within the context of a religious and especially Christian culture. Not only has our culture become secular, but at the same time, another great religious tradition is increasingly present. Our analysis has been rather positive. Secularization is by no means enemy number one for faith and religion. However, the danger is far from imaginary that secularization radicalizes into secularism and the tendency is very real to privatize everything that is religion as much as possible and thus neutralize it.

It is from this question that I want to think further about the Church and about our faith communities: reflecting on their presence and mission within such a changed society. Which pastoral approach is most appropriate? What is the basic pastoral attitude because the challenges are not minor? How do we proclaim the gospel at a time when there is a call for respect for other beliefs and for interreligious dialogue? How do we, as a Church, situate ourselves in a secular and pluralistic society? These are questions that have everything to do with the future of the Church. The analysis has shown that the Church and Christianity have no choice but to situate themselves within the context of a secular and pluralistic culture. But the question that remains is whether they can and may do so from their own self-understanding? Is the Church doing it because it can't do anything else? Or does the Church do it because it is also arising from its own self-understanding or identity? Only in the latter case can the Church accept the secular situation from its own faith and therefore wholeheartedly. So, can it really reconcile itself to the changed situation or does it eventually have to try to turn it around in some way? To answer that question, we must first think about why there is such a thing as a Church. Why Church? Why is it there and what is its mission? Here we leave the realm of analysis and begin the theological reflection.

8

God in Search of Humanity

WHY CHURCH? Usually, that question is asked quite sociologically. Then it is not so difficult to answer. A religion simply cannot exist and especially cannot continue to exist if it does not have even a minimal form of organization and structure. Thus, the reason for the Church's existence is often understood as the organizational form of Christianity. In this sense, the Church is indeed indispensable and necessary. If the Church is viewed in this way, it must also constantly adapt itself structurally. It must constantly adapt to the demands of the times and the needs of the people. This is what in this view is mainly meant by the proper functioning of the Church and how it must always renew itself to keep up with the times.

Yet the Church is more than just the organizational form of Christianity. Her reason for being is to look much further and deeper. It has everything to do with God. If we want to know why the Church exists, the question that really matters is, Does God need the Church? That is the ultimate question: Did God want the Church or not?[1]

We are not used to asking a question about the Church in this way. In the first chapter of *Lumen Gentium*, the Dogmatic Constitution on the Church, the Second Vatican Council speaks of the mystery of the Church. That has nothing to do with mystification. It is a way to express that the Church has its origin in the will and desire of God. Such speaking, of course, means moving from the sociological to the theological language game. Of course, for the Church, its organization and structure remain an important matter. But they do get a new and deeper dimension and meaning from this understanding of faith.

Why Church? In the end, there is only one

---

1. For my thoughts on the Church and its mission, I am very indebted to the German exegete and Scripture theologian Gerhard Lohfink. See especially Gerhard Lohfink, *Heeft God de Kerk nodig? Over de theologie van het volk van God* (Gent: Carmelitana, 2001); and *Wie haat Jezus Gemeinde gewollt? Kirche im Kontrast*, rev. ed. (Stuttgart: Katholisches Bibelwerk, 2015).

answer: because God willed it. We may feel a little uncomfortable with such an answer. Doesn't it smell like fundamentalism? Nevertheless, in this way I want to think further about the Church—not that we humans know everything about God and always know what God's will is. Extreme caution is always advised here. The risk is far from imaginary that we take our will for that of God's. God is and remains the mystery beyond all comprehension. God dwells in the inaccessible light (see 1 Tim 6:16).

When we speak of God here, we mean God as the biblical and Christian tradition has enabled us to know God. According to this belief, God has indeed made God known there. Not that there is nothing else to say about God and about the meaning of human existence outside of this tradition. Yet this tradition says something about God that is unique and at the same time of great importance for the human and his or her happiness, even for the salvation of the world and the future of creation. And that something, if I may express myself in this way, consists in God looking for humankind, that we are not insignificant but are worth everything for God, that God loves us. It is the heart of our faith. It may sound familiar to Christian ears. But it's far from obvious.

We will never understand what God has seen in us. God doesn't need us to be who God is. What could we give God that God doesn't already have? Why did God want this creation? Why so much love? There is no answer to those questions. In the end, love always remains incomprehensible. All true love is gratuitous. How much more than God's love!

> What are human beings that you are
>> mindful of them,
>> mortals that you care for them?
> Yet you have made them a little lower
>> than God,
>> and crowned them with glory and
>> honor. (Ps 8:4–5)

But if it is true that God is really looking for humankind. If there really is this desire in God to meet and share, then it is there that the origin of the Church and its raison d'être must be sought. And this is not just about the Church. This love of God is ultimately about the life and happiness of every human being. We all know from experience that it is communion, love, and solidarity that make life worth living. How much more so when this is in communion with God.

9

God Wants to Share Life

SCRIPTURE TESTIFIES that God has made God known. He has penetrated the inaccessible light, broken the silence. Not to give us some insight or secret knowledge, but to say how much God loves us and how much creation is dear to God's heart. Love is not just the reason why God wants to make God known. It is also the very content of God's revelation.

This is how God has made God known: not as the nameless origin or explanation of all that exists, but as the Creator. God is not only the one who gives life, but also the one who wants to share it with us. That is the great desire of God—

God's plan of salvation: to be with us, to be known, accepted, and loved by us. Creation and revelation are focused on this one goal: the covenant. It is no coincidence that Deuteronomy 6:4–5 expresses the heart of Scripture: "Hear, O Israel: The Lord is our God, the Lord alone. You shall love the Lord your God with all your heart, and with all your soul, and with all your might." When this love of God is abstracted, the Church loses all meaning and its reason for existence.

It is striking that the Bible does not begin with the story of the call of the people of God nor with the foundation of the Church. The Bible begins with the story of creation. The first man involved is neither Abraham nor Moses, but Adam. Adam: that is the human person, humanity. Theologically, this is of capital importance. The significance of those first eleven chapters of the Book of Genesis cannot be overstated. Following this, the story of the call of God's people and of the Church begins. The story of a private people who occasionally give the impression of being almost insignificant, a *petite histoire*. But the ultimate perspective has never been forgotten: the world, creation. This universal perspective will never be forgotten in Scripture. Those first eleven chapters are not just meant as an introduction. They form the lasting background of everything that will be told and said afterward. There will never be the people of God or the Church without reference to the peoples of the world.

What God ultimately has in mind is not directly God's people or the Church. What God has in mind from the beginning, and what will always remain the perspective, is creation, the world, humanity. In the end, when all will be accomplished, it is not the Church that will be saved but creation. What interests God is not so much that there is also room in society for religion, and especially the only true religion. What God wants is for humans to be allowed to live, in the full sense of the word. That creation, that unimaginable experiment, may succeed! As Jesus puts it, "I came that they may have life, and have it abundantly" (John 10:10). It is the certainty and the hope that run like a thread throughout Scripture: what God has begun, God will complete. No wonder that in the last pages of Scripture it is again about creation, but now in the form of completion. It is the vision of the Apocalypse: "a new heaven and a new earth" (Rev 21:1). In God's loving plan of salvation, God does not have a particular religion in mind, but creation and all of humanity.

This is God's purpose. If God created the world and if God called us into existence, it was out of love. God, who is the mystery of love, willed the other: to give, to share and to love. Now, one must realize that this love of God for creation does not depend on the consciousness that people have of it. Even if no human person in the world had knowledge of God and no one knew of God's love for this world, it would still be true that God loves this world and that this is the only grounds for our existence.

But—again for an inexplicable reason—God does not want to love just in secret and in anonymity. Love is indeed gratuitous, yet it reaches out and longs for love. That's what makes love so vulnerable. God does not only want to love; he also wants to be known and loved. That is the fundamental reason why God has turned to us, revealed Godself, and made God known. It turns out to be God's greatest joy to be known, praised, thanked, and loved by God's own creation. God and human are there for each other's happiness, for the covenant with each other. It is in this relationship and in the answer to that love that the human person finds his or her true destiny and happiness.

10

God Gathers a People

BUT HOW CAN GOD get people to love God and want to enter a covenant with God? What can God do so that the human hears God's voice and opens the door for God? How can God find faith and love again? Of course, not by forcing us. Love is suffocated where coercion and fear reign. God did not create us in such a way that we have no choice but to believe in God. That, of course, would have solved many pastoral problems! But what is the point of such a belief? It wouldn't even deserve that name. That is precisely our human condition: the human is not born a believer. Tertullian said it all: *Fiunt, non nascuntur christiani* (*Apologeticum* 18,4). One is not born a Christian; one must become a Christian. Faith and love presuppose freedom; and God is the first to guarantee and respect that freedom. It is the greatness of God and the secret of God's love that God has called into existence a being who can also reject God.

If God seeks us and wants to enter into relationship with us, then there is only one way for God: God must ask us. God must knock at our door. As Christ puts it, "I am standing at the door, knocking; if you hear my voice and open the door, I will come in to you" (Rev 3:20). How delicate is this word of Christ. God doesn't come in without knocking. And even then, God's voice must be heard. God doesn't force the door. God is not self-imposing. God knocks and God waits for an answer to be given. Like the angel waiting for Mary's fiat.

But God doesn't knock on every door at the same time. There is not a spectacular miracle by which God convinces everyone of God's presence. There is not a miracle by which God would be recognized as self-evident once and for good and by which all faith would become superfluous. That is not the way God has chosen. Without freedom, God would never find what God seeks:

an ally with whom God can share life in love and thus in freedom.

There is no other way for God: God had to start somewhere. God started knocking on a door somewhere. This is what Sacred Scripture testifies: God started with Abraham; or at least Abraham is the first to have heard the voice and opened the door. As a result, Abraham has become the father of all believers. And from the beginning about him it was said, "In you all the families of the earth shall be blessed" (Gen 12:3).

With the call of Abraham begins a long history that tells the story in Scripture from the twelfth chapter of the Book of Genesis. After all, Abraham did not remain alone. He has become a people. For many centuries, men and women after him have learned to believe in God and live in God's covenant. There have been moments of great crisis over the course of a long history. Faith never becomes self-evident. There is always the risk of infidelity, the temptation to honor other gods, gods that one makes oneself, and always the temptation to be like the other peoples. But again and again, prophets rose to recall the time when the whole love story with God had begun. To call for repentance and to encourage and be trusting people again.

But "when the fullness of time had come, God sent his Son" (Gal 4:4). This long history was fulfilled in the coming of the Messiah, Christ the Lord, who died and rose again. The New Testament testifies to this. It is in that conviction and faith that the Church came into being. In Christ, God has gathered a new people. New because now not only those who belonged to the people of God's first election, but also those who come from the many nations and profess Christ as Messiah and Son of God, cleansed in the water of baptism. So that long history continues, the long history that began with Abraham. God calls constantly and gathers God's people: the children of Abraham, the people of God's first love, and the communion of the Church, the Body of Christ.

Why does God want a people? Why does God gather men and women into the communion of the Church? The answer to that question shows us what the Church really is and what it is called to do. We have already emphasized it: God desires that there are places on this earth where the door is opened for God and God is already recognized and loved, where God can already share and live in communion with those who are God's creatures.

They are places where the redemption of the world is already beginning. They are places where, with all limitations and fragility, something of what God already had in mind when God created the world and humankind becomes visible. It is God's desire that those places are visible so that all can see and hear what is said and experienced there. God wants to make salvation known to all people, not through convenient persuasion mechanisms nor through indoctrination, but through the living faith and the interceding presence of a faith community. There is no compulsion or moral pressure. It is in complete freedom that people are called. People can be touched or fascinated by what they hear and see, by identifying what it does to people when they share their lives with God and how faith changes their lifestyle and makes it more human. It is in this way that God wants to make God known as a source of salvation and blessing for the whole world. As Pope Francis puts it in imitation of Benedict XVI, "The Church grows not through proselytism but through 'attraction.'"[1]

So, what can be seen in those places? What's going on there? And above all, what does God want to happen there? They are first and foremost places where God's voice—God's word—is

---

1. Pope Francis, *Evangelii Gaudium*, no. 14.

heard. It is no coincidence that this is precisely the first and great commandment throughout the biblical tradition, both in the Old and New Testaments: "Hear, O Israel!" (Deut 6:4). As Jesus says of his disciples, "The sheep follow him because they know his voice" (John 10:4). Just as Mary, the sister of Lazarus, is said to have chosen the better part (see Luke 10:42).

Already from a purely human perspective, this is one of the deepest desires of every human being: to be able to express what he or she has on his or her heart and to be listened to. What a source of pain and sadness it is if that is not possible—if one remains locked in oneself. What pain and sorrow are experienced when one speaks in vain and is not listened to. It's perhaps one of the hardest things: being able to listen. How often does it happen: you have only just started speaking, you have only said a few words, and they already think they understand you and start expressing what they think you wanted to say!

That is the primary reason God longs for such places: to speak and find a listening ear. Not to tell us anything and everything, but to say, in so many ways and in so many circumstances, that God loves us. To say what is in God's heart, to share. That is what God desires: people who are receptive to

God's presence, sensitive to God's intentions, listening to what God has to say to them. They are places where one learns to believe and love. For faith is never just the logical conclusion of reasoning. As Paul puts it: faith comes from listening—*fides ex auditu!* (Rom 10:17).

Yet God does not only desire places where God can already speak and where God is listened to. God also hopes that God's self-expression and open heart are not in vain. God demands a response—an answer that is given in freedom and one that is truly heartfelt. The Church is therefore a place of prayer. For prayer is always the answer to the one who first sought contact and who spoke first. Not only the personal prayer, but also and primarily community prayer, the prayer of the Church, liturgical prayer. It is the prayer of those who have been called together by God just for this purpose: to listen to God's word and then to address the word to God and answer God. That prayer establishes communion with God, but also communion with each other.

This should never be overlooked when looking for the Church's raison d'être. Prayer is part of the reason for its existence and its mission. When God makes God known and speaks, God always expresses God's love and friendship. In its

Constitution on the Divine Revelation, the Second Vatican Council put it simply and beautifully: that God addresses us in love "as to friends."[2] That is precisely what God is looking for: communion and friendship. That is why that same Council says of the efficacy of the liturgy that "no other action of the Church can equal its efficacy by the same title and to the same degree."[3]

It is therefore not surprising that the liturgy of the Eucharist has such a central meaning in the faith and life of the Church. It is the prayer par excellence, the great prayer of thanksgiving of the whole Church in communion with Christ, the Lord. Like any liturgy, it is a celebration of the covenant. As it happens in every family, on big occasions one gathers regularly to have a meal together, but always for the same reason: to gratefully celebrate the joy and happiness of their communal bond. And so too is the profound meaning of the Eucharist and of every liturgy: celebrating the new and eternal covenant. Every liturgy testifies to the joy of being able to abide in God's presence, *coram Deo*. A community of faith is not just a place where God's word is listened to. But it is also the place where one is always, again and again,

2. Second Vatican Council, *Dei Verbum*, no. 2.
3. Second Vatican Council, *Sacrosanctum Concilium*, no. 7.

more deeply connected to God who gathers us and also with each other. We recall the words of Jesus: "That they may all be one. As you, Father, are in me and I in you, may they also be in us" (John 17:21). There is not only the Word but also the Sacrament and especially the sacrament par excellence, the most holy sacrament of the Eucharist.

Yet listening and answering are not enough because you don't just answer love with words. God can only feel at home in places where God also finds something of God's lifestyle: where that which is considered important also concerns God and where God has not spoken in vain. Otherwise, God feels like a stranger in God's own home. Already the prophets of the First Covenant warned against a cult without a heart for one's fellow humans.

> What to me is the multitude of your
>   sacrifices?
>   says the LORD....
>   Learn to do good,
> seek justice,
>   rescue the oppressed,
> defend the orphan,
>   plead for the widow. (Isa 1:11, 17)

At the end of the Sermon on the Mount, where Jesus calls even for love for the enemy, he says, "Not everyone who says to me 'Lord! Lord!' will enter the kingdom of heaven, but only the one who does the will of my Father in heaven" (Matt 7:21).

Love is a verb. True love always manifests itself in deeds. This applies to the love among people, but also to the love of God. One cannot meet the living God and at the same time remain the same as one was. The encounter touches us in our deepest life options. Whoever shares life with God, in love and in suffering, in good and in bad days, also becomes more and more sensitive to what God cares about. God's commandments are not just obligations. They are covenant requirements in all truth. That is why the lifestyle of a faith community wants to be like that of God.

It is a lifestyle in which one learns to give and share and where fraternity and solidarity are the supreme law. Not to be mindful of just one's own benefit and profit, but to be concerned for and about the other, for the poor, and for those who are also in need. In his Letter to the Philippians, Paul exhorts Christians to regard the other higher than oneself so that the same disposition may reign in them that was in Christ. For, he says,

Who, though he was in the form of God,
    did not regard equality with God
    as something to be exploited,
but emptied himself,
    taking the form of a slave,
    being born in human likeness.
      (Phil 2:6–7)

As Jesus expresses in John's Gospel, "By this everyone will know that you are my disciples, if you have love for one another" (John 13:35).

11

A Sign of Salvation for the World

AFTER ALL THAT has been said so far, there remains an inevitable question: What about those who do not belong to the Church community? What about the world and humanity? Is there no salvation outside the Church?

We have already made it clear that what God has in mind is not first and foremost the Church itself but the world, God's creation. When God calls and chooses God's people, it is not because God leaves the world to its fate. Then the election would not really be understood. God is and remains the Creator and Lord of heaven and earth. What God has begun with creation, God will also complete. In his Letter to the Christians of Rome, Paul writes "in hope that the creation itself will be set free from its bondage to decay and will obtain the freedom of the glory of the children of God" (Rom 8:20–21). The ultimate perspective is not the Church but a new creation, freed from the power of sin and death. That is precisely why God needs the Church. The election of God's people does not mean that God has only contempt for those who do not belong to it. One can understand election only out of God's love for this world and for the salvation of creation.

Certainly, what the Church and every ecclesial community must first do are to ensure that God finds a place where God can already be received. They do so by coming together to listen to God's word, to celebrate the covenant with God gratefully, and by being creative in seeking ways of fraternity and solidarity. But precisely by doing so, the Church also wants to say something to the citizens of the society in which it lives. As a Church, it is always a sign to the outside world. It testifies to God's presence amid this world and to God's great link with humanity.

There is a close and indivisible bond between what the Church experiences inwardly and what it radiates outwardly. For if God calls and gathers the Church, if God needs it, it is not only because God would already find a place where God can live in communion with people, but also because God wants to make God heard and known to every human being—to say that God loved this world to the end and therefore sent God's only Son. It is not through a publicity campaign, but primarily through its existence and presence that the Church is a sign and sacrament of God's love for all people.

It is an extremely important but also extremely delicate task for the Church to ensure that this is always the ultimate meaning of everything the Church says and does: that the Church does everything it can to ensure that it does not give rise to misunderstanding on this point. Of course, through what the Church says or does, it can also mean many other things, things that have nothing to do with the Church's mission or that can even obscure it. The Church will also be a sign of contradiction if necessary. But by what the Church says or does, it must not give rise to any misunderstanding about the ultimate reason for its existence or about the purpose of the Church's mission.

That is precisely the risk and danger when Christianity plays the role of a cultural religion.

Then other interests will also come into play. Then the Church risks folding back on itself and, above all, trying to save and preserve itself. Then one begins to behave like one of the religions and then competes with the other. Just as was always the temptation of Israel to be like the other nations. One then forgets why it is ultimately doable: that this world touches God's heart and that God is the source of salvation and blessing for all people. For example, we read in John's Gospel, "For God so loved the world that he gave his only Son" (John 3:16). Paul adds, "He did not withhold his own Son, but gave him up for all of us" (Rom 8:32).

The Church must not fold back on itself. It has a commission from God to the outside world. Pope Francis constantly warns us against an over-confident and self-involved attitude. He speaks of a dynamic of exodus "to step out of ourselves and go to the other, to sow ever more and more."[1] He speaks of a Church *en sortie*: "to pull away from our own comforts to courageously face all who are removed from the faith in the light of the Gospel."[2] The Church cannot understand itself except in its relationship to the world in which it lives. It is intimately connected to that world, in

---

1. Pope Francis, *Evangelii Gaudium*, no. 21.
2. *Evangelii Gaudium* 21.

solidarity with the fate of all humanity. It is in and for the world that it is called to be the Church and the people of God.

Therefore, all attempts to privatize the faith are an attack on the very heart of the Christian faith. It is the mission itself of the Church that privatized faith questions. The Church cannot understand itself as an institution concerned solely with its own religious problems. Christianity understands itself as a religion that is relevant to the real life of people, to the task of living together and thus building society. When Dietrich Bonhoeffer argues in his *Letters and Papers from Prison*[3] for what he calls a nonreligious Christianity, this is what he means: no to a Christianity that would only be pertinent to the religious dimension of human existence, but not to the real life of people in all its dimensions, nor to the search for a more humane and just society. Christianity is not mere spiritualism.

The gospel is a word of life. A word about humankind and human happiness, about the world and the future of humankind. The Church in no way seeks the seclusion of the ghetto. It is not a club of like-minded people nor a cult. The

---

3. Dietrich Bonhoeffer, *Letters and Papers from Prison.* The original German edition *Widerstand und Ergebung* was first published in 1951 by Kaiser Verlag München. The book was composed by Eberhardt Bethge, his friend and biographer, from letters written by Bonhoeffer in Tegel Prison in Berlin.

Church shares the love and suffering of people and of this world. That is why it wants to be present in society. In that sense, the Church is a public institution. It does not address a separate group. Its door is open to everyone. It does not complacently lock itself in upon itself. But rather, the Church wants to be a sign to the outside world and address every human being. And if it happens that the Church loses all relevance to the outside world, then it should not simply resign itself to that. It is precisely then that the Church must question itself and see whether it is truly fulfilling the calling that God has entrusted to it.

Today, the search for a proper relationship with the world and society is a delicate matter for the Church. We live in a society marked by secularity and pluralism. It is our duty to live together with respect for others and for their convictions. Dialogue with the world and interreligious dialogue are extremely important. It is in this context that the Church also wants to make its voice heard. It is in this context that Church communities also want to radiate outward. No pastoral ministry is worthy of the name if it is not based on respect for others and their freedom.

The Church has a universal mission and yet it retains its own particularity. It is neither the world nor the whole of humankind. The Church is the people of God who live amid the nations. It is by no means the Church's task to regain the status and position that it had managed to maintain until the recent past. What God asks of the Church is that there be places where God can already live with us. Places, not just here and there, but wherever people live. Places where people live in a covenant with God. Places where we learn to love as God has loved this world without end. That is our way of being present in society. It is in this sense that the Church is called to be a sign of God's love and of God's great humanity.

12

A Chosen People

THE CRISIS OF THE Church in the West is usually associated with the shrinking of our communities. The number of vocations for an ecclesiastical ministry or for religious life no longer has any real comparison with what we had come to know earlier last century. In the media, it is generally regarded as a sign that we are gradually experiencing the end of Western Christianity. The facts are obvious. But it is important to understand those facts and the entire process of change correctly. A page has been turned. It's not like it used to be. But is it the end?

It has already been discussed that the Church and the world do not coincide. Already the analysis of the situation of the Church in the West has shown the ambiguity of a society that is itself Christian. We have already pointed out the danger of religious cultures. It is not for nothing that the rise of modernity is inextricably linked to the liberation from ecclesiastical patronage. Our theological reflection has already shown that even based on the Christian faith itself, the Church cannot indeed think of itself as coinciding with the world or society.

Yet very often, both inside and outside the Church, Christianity continues to be seen as a cultural religion. The fact that the Church has lost this status in modern society and is thus increasingly confronted with its own limitations and particularity is understood as regression or even as the beginning of the end. In the subconscious there remains a persistent conviction: the Christian faith tends by itself to become the religion of everyone. Only then is Christianity truly itself. If that is not the case, then it cannot accept the facts. Of course, there may be circumstances in which those facts must be accepted. This can happen in places where the Church is a threatened minority and is persecuted, as is the case in the Middle East and in many other places today. Or where the Church lives in a country or continent where another religion is a cultural religion, such as in Muslim countries or in Asia. In these cases, one has no choice but to reconcile oneself with the actual situation. But then it is the circumstances that necessitate it. But the question is whether the Church can and may do so if circumstances do not force it to do so.

Hence the enduring questions: Can Christianity see and appreciate modern culture, secular and nonreligious, as the normal situation in which it must fulfill its mission? Or should it continue to see that situation as the great danger and join forces to turn the tide? Can the Church accept and appreciate its own limitations or does the Church's universal mission mean that the ultimate objective is the Christianization of the whole of society?

Israel and the Jewish people will naturally be spoken of as a separate and private people. Israel also understands itself this way: as the people God has chosen from all nations, a people who belong to him in a special way. "The LORD has taken you and brought you out of the iron-smelter, out of Egypt, to become a people of his very own possession, as you are now" (Deut 4:20). Ever since the time of the exile until today, it has been the vocation of Judaism to live among the other peoples, living in the scattering, in the Diaspora.

Of course, one can convert to Judaism. It is not a closed group. Yet Judaism does not have the desire to become the faith of the peoples. For that, it is too aware of its own calling and mission, and also of its own limitations and particularity.

But very often and just as naturally, it is stated that this is precisely how it is different from the Church and Christianity: whereas Judaism is a separate and private people, the Church is universal. It is true that whereas the Church was a Church of Jews in its very beginning, it also very quickly opened itself up to non-Jews. It was not circumcision that was a condition for it to belong to God's people, but only the belief in Jesus as Lord and Messiah and baptism in his name. This is how the Church understands itself as the new Israel, the people that God has called and chosen from Jews and Gentiles. But please note that it remains a people who have been called and chosen by God as God's special property, as the community that belongs to God in a special way.

This openness to those who do not belong to the people of God's first election became possible precisely by Christ's redemptive work. But that openness in no way prevents this new people of God, composed of Jews and Gentiles, just like

Israel itself, from being a people set apart and not encompassing the entire world population. The Church, too, is called to live among the nations.

In the face of particularity and especially in the face of the concept of election, we feel very uncomfortable. Only what is universal and applies to everyone, it seems, can claim to be the truth. Particularity smells of particularism, election to superiority and arrogance. For Jewish and biblical awareness, however, this is not the case. Election does indeed mean that you receive a special mission, but not that you are more than the others. When you are called, it is not because of special qualities, nor does it in any way confer on you a privileged status. "It was not because you were more numerous than any other people that the LORD set his heart on you and chose you—for you were the fewest of all peoples" (Deut 7:7). In the parable of the Pharisee and the tax collector, Jesus teaches that you should not think that you are better than the others. Knowing oneself as "chosen" in that sense finds no mercy with God.

If there was any particular reason why Israel was called, it was only because it was in need, living in tribulation, and at the mercy of injustice and despair. That is also the way the Book of Exodus understands election. Those words are the very heart of the biblical experience of God: "I have observed the misery of my people who are in Egypt; I have heard their cry on account of their taskmasters. Indeed, I know their sufferings, and I have come down to deliver them from the Egyptians" (Exod 3:7-8). In the beautiful parable with Ezekiel, it is again God who speaks in those terms about the vocation of God's people:

> No eye pitied you, to do any of these things for you out of compassion for you; but you were thrown out in the open field, for you were abhorred on the day you were born. I passed by you, and saw you flailing about in your blood. As you lay in your blood, I said to you, "Live! and grow up like a plant of the field." (Ezek 16:5-7)

Election is always gratuitous and does not imply any privileged status. It never implies, therefore, that God leaves others and the world to their fate. Israel is called and chosen precisely as a sign that God loves this world, a sign of salvation for all nations. In a prophecy from Isaiah, the Lord addresses this word to his people:

It is too light a thing that you should be
    my servant
  to raise up the tribes of Jacob
  and to restore the survivors of Israel;
I will give you as a light to the nations,
  that my salvation may reach to the
    end of the earth. (Isa 49:6)

What has been said above about the election of Israel also applies to the vocation of the Church. Nowhere in the New Testament is it even suggested that the notions of election and particularity would no longer apply to it. In the First Epistle of Peter, it is said quite clearly:

But you are a chosen race, a royal priesthood, a holy nation, God's own people, in order that you may proclaim the mighty acts of him who called you out of darkness into his marvelous light.

Once you were not a people,
  but now you are God's people;
once you had not received mercy,
  but now you have received mercy.
    (1 Pet 2:9–10)

The entire letter, by the way, is addressed "To the exiles of the Dispersion" (1:1). That is the normal condition of the Church and of the Christian: living in the Diaspora.

Today we are becoming more aware of the particularity and limitations of the Church—a Church that is therefore, as a matter of course, numerically smaller. We should not experience this as a threat.

For centuries, Christianity here in the West has had the status of a cultural religion. But that is not its self-evident status. Historical circumstances have led to this. Obviously, we live in a secular society. It is normal that the Church does not represent the whole of the population, and it would greatly damage its credibility if the Church were to pursue that position in the current situation.

Yet the Church's limitations and particularity in no way call into question the Church's universal mission. God's grace and love do not only go out to the people of the Church. As a separate and particular community, the Church is a sign of God's universal love and of God's universal will for salvation. As a sacrament, it means precisely that salvation is not only to be found in the Church and that God is not active in just the space of the Church.

In the Constitution on the Church, the Second Vatican Council testified to the extent to which God's salvation extends beyond the boundaries of the visible Church.[1] First, the Jewish people are mentioned, the people of God's first election. "For the gifts and the calling of God are irrevocable" (Rom 11:29). Also mentioned are the Muslims who share the faith of Abraham and worship, with us, in the one and merciful God. But equally, those who do not know God through any fault of their own and live according to their conscience are mentioned. All of them are said not to live without God's grace and that God's providence helps them in all that is necessary for their salvation.

To understand the mission of the Church and the Church's place in society, understanding the Church as sacrament is crucial. The Council also places great emphasis on this. "In Christ, the Church is, as it were, the sacrament—that is, the sign and instrument—of intimate union with God and of the unity of all humankind."[2] A sacrament is a visible and real sign of God's grace and of God's love. That is precisely the mission of the Church: to be a true sign of God's grace—not just of God's grace for itself—but to be a sign of God's grace and

---

1. Second Vatican Council, *Lumen Gentium*, no. 16.
2. *Lumen Gentium* 1.

love for this world and for all humankind. As a sign, it is limited and private. But what it means has universal meaning, and it concerns the whole world and creation.

That is the very way in which God, according to Scripture, always deals with us and makes God known. If God were to meet us in an overwhelming revelation that spares nothing or no one, the Church would indeed not be limited and private, but would encompass the entire world population. Then God would not have to give a sign of God's love. God would have been forced on all. But then, in that case, one could hardly speak of love and covenant. And also, no longer of faith.

13

A Missionary Church

NEVERTHELESS, it remains a pressing question whether the Church can reconcile itself with its limitations and particularity. Isn't it tending toward universality? Is it not the Church's mission to bring as many people as possible into contact with the gospel? Is not the Church's mission, especially in a secularized society, to be missionary? As Paul so poignantly writes, "If I proclaim the gospel, this gives me no ground for boasting, for an obligation is laid on me, and woe to me if I do not proclaim the gospel!" (1 Cor 9:16).

Of course, that question can only be answered positively. The Church is not a closed community. It is the sacrament of salvation for the world. The Church cannot understand itself unless it is involved in the world. The Church is not there for itself alone. It is a city on the hill (see Matt 5:14), light on the lampstand (see Matt 5:15), a signal for the peoples (see Isa 11:10). Even where the Church is silent or silenced, the Church proclaims the gospel just by the fact that it exists and is present. A Church that folds back on itself loses its own substance and its reason for existence. A Church that no longer missions, no longer radiates outward, and no longer attracts newcomers, is a Church that shrivels inward. Then, it is only trying to survive and save itself.

The real question, therefore, is not so much whether the Church can maintain its current membership, as much as that might be a concern. The real question is whether the Church can also attract new people. This shows the vitality of a Church: not so much by the number that one still maintains (!), but whether a person who is fully integrated into this secular culture can be touched by the power and beauty of the gospel: how the gospel can answer in all truth the great questions of humankind, to what degree it points the way to a good and human life, and how much it also brings light and hope for the great social challenges facing humanity.

So, there can be no doubt that the Church will always proclaim the gospel. It is the Church's essence and the meaning of its existence. Church is mission. The fact that the Church can receive new Christians into its community will always be a sign of its vitality and health. However, it must be added immediately that it will not always be able and necessary to do so in the same circumstances and in the same way. We already talked about evangelization here in the West after antiquity, which gradually made Christianity the cultural religion. We have already pointed out how historical circumstances made this Christianization possible and desirable. But historical circumstances are variable and not eternal. In the meantime, they have changed, and we live here in a secular and pluralistic society.

In these new circumstances, continuing to see the Church's mission as the task of Christianizing society can only lead to great impasses. It would greatly damage the credibility of the Church if it were really the Church's intention to put an end to this secular and pluralistic society in order to make it a religious, and in this case, a Christian culture again. It would then have to compete with the other religions with the conviction that they should disappear. Such an attitude or strategy would then have nothing to do with the gospel, but everything to do with an extreme derailment of Christianity.

Missionary work does not necessarily mean the Christianization of society. Missionary work should not be confused with the restoration of a homogeneous Christian civilization. The Church is not called to become the world itself and to take the whole of society into its womb gradually. The Church is the community of Christians, not the gathering of global populations. Thus, in the Gospels, a distinction is so often made between the student group and the crowd. In the Sermon on the Mount, Jesus addresses his disciples explicitly, but in such a way that the crowd also hears it (see Matt 5:1–2). The Church is indeed called to be a sign of God's love in word and deed within the world.

The blending of Church and world is not a historical, but an eschatological reality. As long as the world lasts, the Church will live "scattered." In a speech at Rabat cathedral in Morocco in 2019, Pope Francis said,

> The problem is not that we are not numerous but that we would have nothing more to do with it, that we become

salt that no longer has the taste of the Gospel—that is the problem!—or that we are a lamp that no longer illuminates anything (cf. Matt 5:13-15). I think the problem arises when we Christians get caught up in the idea that we can only mean something if we are the total mass and occupy all space.[1]

It benefits both the Church and society when the Church recognizes the boundary between the Church and the world. But that does not mean to withdraw from society and lose solidarity with the world. On the contrary, the recognition of one's own border is done out of respect for the world, and it is ultimately also out of respect for the Church itself. Precisely to the extent that the Church knows about that boundary, the Church knows about itself and about its own identity. You can only mean something to someone if you are someone yourself. We already stated that you can only radiate outward what is going on inside.

But does the Church not have the mission to proclaim the gospel to all peoples, indeed to all creation? Is that not what Jesus asks at the end of

---

1. Pope Francis, "Pas de prosélytisme pour la mission," *La Documentation Catholique* 2535 (July 2019): 80.

the Gospel of Matthew? "Go therefore and make disciples of all nations" (Matt 28:19). That is indeed the Church's mission: to make known to all the gospel of God's love. No one should be excluded. No person, of any race, color, language, or origin, no one from any continent or nationality, or any religious affiliation, is beyond God's grace. The Church is not everything, but the Church is itself a people in the midst of the peoples. But it is a people called from all peoples. At this point, there are no restrictions. That is the universality of the Church's mission.

That universality also refers to the Church's catholicity. It is a Church that is spread all over the world. As a particular group in society, it is not a cult. Therefore, it is the Church's calling to be everywhere, wherever possible. Also in the peripheries, as Pope Francis rightly says. Not only geographically but also existentially. Everywhere and in all living conditions. Especially where humanity is threatened, the Church will be present and bear witness in word and deed to God's nearness, to God's love and compassion.

And certainly, the Church must not limit itself to its own inner circle, to those who regularly gather in it—even when the Church withdraws to itself: a complacent attitude that shows little openness. The archbishop of Lille rightly writes in a pastoral letter,

> Yes, it is those who are farthest from us, those who know the Church from the outside only by the image, positive or negative, that the media bring, even those who are so hurt that they no longer want to hear from us, those who have never really heard of Jesus and the Gospel, those who live in contexts that we know so little about—in the scientific world and in that of the most advanced technologies and many others where we have so little presence and our input is so weak.[2]

There is no place in this world, no country, no continent, no category of people, and no situation in which or from whom one could say, "Oh, leave those people alone. There need be no Church here. Here the gospel has nothing to offer. Christianity may still be good in countries where it was once brought. It belongs to the historical and cultural patrimony. But you should not bother other

---

2. Mgr. Laurent Ulrich, "Serviteurs joyeux et créatifs de la misson de l'Eglisie," Pastoral Letter, March 2020, 8.

peoples, countries, or continents which have their own religious traditions." With such views, the Church does indeed withdraw into itself. Then, the Church ceases to be missionary. Then, the Church also slowly faces its end.

So the question is not whether the Church should be missionary. The question is how the Church should be missionary. How can the Church understand its mission in a secular and pluralistic culture? In Asia, Christians live in societies defined by very ancient and great religious traditions. Others live in Muslim countries. These are situations where the Church is by no means everything, but quite the contrary. The Church is by no means in crisis, and not whining either, let alone issuing condemnation because society itself is not Christian. And although the Church may be limited in its activities by these circumstances, the Church is not prevented from being fully and vitally present in these societies. Mutatis mutandis also applies to our situation here in the West. It's the basic questions I'm thinking about in this chapter. How can the Church be missionary without denying the rights of modern culture? How can the Church be missionary without striving for a re-Christianization of society itself?

My answer to these questions is twofold. First, we must not condemn this modern society for no longer being homogeneously Christian. We can and must wholeheartedly accept it in its secularity and pluralism. We therefore do not need to assimilate and endorse all that this secular culture has to offer. But we are citizens of this society and have integrated ourselves into this culture as believers and as a Church. We are children of our time, not of a past cultural phase. We share as well in the big questions and challenges of such a culture.

Therefore, we must not withdraw from such a society and build our own separate world. We want no closed and self-withdrawn Church, no privatized faith, no otherworldly Christianity. But at the same time, we must be a Church that bears witness to the gospel and makes its voice heard in the great ethical and social debates in which the humanity and the future of our planet are at stake. That's what I mean by being present in society.

But—and this is the second part of my answer to the questions—we have to be present in our own way. That means concretely by being Church, by doing what we are called to do, by seeking God and listening to God's word, by answering God in prayer and liturgy. We do this in gratitude and praise, in mutual love, and in solidarity with those who are in need in any way. As it says so beautifully in the Acts of the Apostles about the earliest Church in Jerusalem, "They devoted themselves to the apostles' teaching and fellowship, to the breaking of bread and the prayers" (Acts 2:42).

It is interesting to see how Paul exercised his mission. He saw it as his task to establish Christian communities all over the place on his mission trips. When this had happened, he did not stay there until the whole city had become Christian. Once a Christian community was there, he moved on to create communities elsewhere as well. At the end of his letter to the Christians of Rome, he writes, "Thus I make it my ambition to proclaim the good news, not where Christ has already been named" (Rom 15:20). There, Paul writes that he is planning on going to Spain. But on the way, he first wants to visit the church community in Rome. To announce and prepare for his visit, he writes them his letter. But strangely enough, Paul sees his task in the eastern part of the Empire as complete: "So that from Jerusalem and as far around as Illyricum I have fully proclaimed the good news of Christ....But now, with no further place for me in these regions, I desire, as I have for many years, to come to you" (Rom 15:19, 23).

It is remarkable that Paul sees his task as complete. This is only possible because he sees missionary work as the founding of local communities. Once that community is established, its very presence and the way in which it develops further is the way in which the proclamation of the gospel takes place. But that, of course, presupposes that that community does not fold back on itself. However, the community must effectively radiate to the outside what can be experienced inside.

In the pre-Constantine period, the growth and spread of Christianity was not the result of a strategic missionary plan, but rather the effect of its presence and its conspicuousness. In our contemporary circumstances, in a secular culture, it is of great importance that the Church and Church communities take great care for the authenticity of their experience of faith. Always in the knowledge that it is precisely because of this that the Church can radiate outward and touch people. It is a fallacy to think that the Church should not attach too much importance to inner-church pastoral care, to have more time and energy to come out and convince others. What would you have to preach to those others, and how could you convince those others if you could not refer to places where what you preach is actually lived, no matter how imperfect? It is not the case that, on the one hand, we are Church, people of God and Body of Christ, and on the other hand, we also have the additional mission of being a sacrament for the world. It is precisely by being Church that we are a sacrament to the world. It is through what there is to experience within the Church community that the Church can be relevant to the outside world.

Of course, the Church can take missionary initiatives and develop missionary methods. But in essence, Church being Church is the method. In the literal sense of the word, it is the way that God has chosen to make God's name and God's love known. It does not do mission. Mission is not one of its activities. The Church is mission; it is the means par excellence that fits perfectly with the way God deals with this world and in which God wants to make God known. If you like someone and want to show it to him or her, then that is a very delicate matter. Love does not want to overwhelm. As Paul puts it, "Love is patient; love is kind; love is not envious or boastful or arrogant or rude. It does not insist on its own way; it is not irritable or resentful" (1 Cor 13:4–5). And certainly, love does not expect an answer that the other only feels obliged to do for some reason or that suits him or her better. This also applies to the Church and to the Church's mission: the Church is long-suffering and clement, not envious. The Church does not love pageantry and doesn't care about appearances. And above all, the Church does not seek itself.

THE TESTIMONY OF THE MONKS OF TIBHIRINE

The Church is not there for itself. It is there to make God's love known. It is the best method and the most appropriate means of achieving this. As a sacrament, it is both a sign and an instrument. The Church speaks and acts. The Church prays and celebrates the liturgy. The Church is close to the person in need, and lives and feels sympathy with the ups and downs of this world. The Church is committed to a more just and humane society. It is not a private club that meets somewhere in secret. The Church is public and visible. Everyone can hear and see what is being said and done. It does not oblige anyone to anything. But it's there. The Church is the place where God's love full of joy and gratitude is confirmed and shared. You can ignore it indifferently. But you can also be affected or addressed by what you hear or see. It doesn't happen through persuasion techniques nor through strategies that get people where we want them to go. For those who believe, all of this is the work of God's grace. And it happens in complete freedom. Only in this way can God find what God has been seeking from the beginning and why it is all for God to do: that God's human creations know and love God and enter into covenant to share life with God.

The film *Of Gods and Men* about the Trappist community of Tibhirine has appealed to and touched many. In the monastery of Tibhirine, nine Cistercian monks lived in harmony with the largely Muslim population of Algeria. There is nothing spectacular to see in it. The monastery also has no strategy to be as up to date as possible. Monks remain themselves in all simplicity. They lead the life of a monk, a life of prayer and labor, a life as much as possible according to the simplicity of the gospel and in community. Like the earliest church of Jerusalem: faithful to the teachings of the apostles; faithful to prayer and the breaking of bread; faithful to the common life, but at the same time with a touching friendship and solidarity with the people outside the monastery, at the risk of their own lives, sharing as much as possible their joy and sorrow, also their fear, because their lives are as threatened as those of the monks themselves. No semblance of any proselytism. Rather, a great and deeply lived reverence for what the people are, for their culture and their faith.

The liturgy is also beautiful and true. Even those who are not familiar with it feel it. Yet here, too, there is no attempt to adapt them to the situation. It speaks for itself: The words of Scripture or the prayers sound new, sometimes surprising. This is not because they were modified or changed, but because of the so vital context in which they are spoken.

I see in the monastery of Tibhirine a paradigm of what the Church can be. Of course, not to turn the whole Church into a monastic community! But in the community of Tibhirine, something of what is the vocation of the Church in our greatly changed society lights up. A modest and smaller Church, living in the Diaspora. It is a Church that is faithful to its faith and uninhibitedly itself. But it is also an open Church, in solidarity with the questions, the joys, and the fears of the people of our time. It is a Church that first radiates the joy and happiness of living in the simplicity of the gospel. It is a Church that bears witness to God's love for all people: a Church and Christians who are committed to a more humane world, to those who are poor, sick, lonely, or in any need. It is a Church for so many who, despite all emancipation and progress, do not count. They are victims of the globalization of indifference.

14

Encounter and Dialogue

W E HAVE ALREADY shown how much the secular character of our culture has fundamentally changed the place of Christianity and the Church, but not made it impossible. On the contrary, we have also demonstrated how this secular culture pushes its own boundaries and has every interest in recognizing those boundaries. It cannot take the place of religion. And even less can a secular culture set itself up as a kind of cultural civil religion. This is precisely to guarantee freedom and to safeguard the democratic character of society, so as not to slip into the exclusive rights of an ideological secularism. Modernity is not itself an institution that can give meaning and direction to our lives and to our coexistence. We have noted that it tells us that we are free and that we must respect each other's freedom, but it does not tell us what to do and what makes our lives worth living. It is precisely at this point that the most important and even necessary place of religions and its social significance is situated.

So far, our primary focus has been on what all this means for the Church and how it can understand its mission in such a context. But every now and then the other religions also came into view. For in essence, this problem does not just concern Christianity and the Church. All religions here in the Western world are faced with the question of their meaning within the context of a secular culture.

During the long period that Christianity was a cultural religion here, of course, the other ancient and great religious traditions also existed, especially Judaism, Islam, and the major Asian religions. But those religions were situated outside the boundaries of Western Christendom. People knew that there were other religions, but not here; the only exception, as we noted, was Judaism. But between Church and Synagogue, the relationship always remained tense, never without the threat of discrimination, exclusion, and persecution.

Through migration, other religions have become part of Western society today. Our society is determined not only by the process of secularization, but also by the growing presence of other religions and especially of Islam. From this angle, too, the question arises as to what this means for Christianity and how the Church can understand its mission in this new context. If the Church is essentially missionary, should it be so in its relationship with the other religions? Is it the Church's task to convince the other religions as well?

We have clarified why it is so important for the Church and for the future of Christianity that the rights and legitimacy of a secular culture be wholeheartedly endorsed. Should this also be done regarding the other religious traditions? This should happen not only because it is a civic duty within a secular and modern society, but for welcomed peace! But should it be done wholeheartedly? Or does the truth of the gospel mean that one must ultimately deny the legitimacy of other religions out of one's own Christian belief?

Just as we asked the question earlier about whether missionary work can be understood as the Christianization of society, here we ask the question whether mission is the same as proselytism. Again, the answer is negative. Here, too, this is an extremely important matter. It is important not only for the Church but also for society itself. Of course, we are not going to go into the whole issue of interreligious dialogue here. However, we want to show how this matter can also help us to understand better our place as a Church in society and our missionary mission: to situate ourselves more correctly in a way that does justice to the other religions and ultimately also to the gospel itself.

The relationship between Judaism and Christianity, between Church and Synagogue, already shows how delicate this issue is. Judaism has a very special meaning for Christianity. The Jewish faith of which the Hebrew Scriptures testify is not another religion for the Christian, but the origin and foundation of the Christian's own faith. Of course, for the Christian, Christ himself remains the key to understanding the Hebrew Scriptures. None other than Christ is the cornerstone (see 1 Pet 2:4–8). But that does not prevent Judaism from having a meaning for the Church that no other religion has for the Church. It was Saint John Paul II who spoke these words in the synagogue of Rome on April 13, 1986:

> The Jewish religion is not completely out-
> side of us, but somehow belongs to our
> religion. We therefore have ties with it
> that we have with no other religion. You
> are our privileged brothers, and in a sense
> one could also say our older brothers.

This is indeed about the significance of Judaism for Christianity and not just about the Christian meaning of the Hebrew Scriptures. The Church knows herself to be the new people of God. But that does not mean that Judaism should cease to exist in the Church's eyes. The Church does not replace the people whom God chose first. The new thing that Christ has brought is precisely that now the Gentiles also have access to the one people of God's promise. We Christians out of paganism are "a wild olive shoot...grafted in their place to share the rich root of the olive tree" (Rom 11:17).

In 2015, the Pontifical Commission for Religious Relations with the Jews published a particularly fine text. The Commission is part of the Pontifical Council for Interreligious Dialogue. It states under number 40 the following:

> The so-called "mission to the Jews" is a
> very delicate and sensitive matter for

Jews because, in their eyes, it involves the very existence of the Jewish people. This question also proves to be awkward for Christians, because for them the universal salvific significance of Jesus Christ and consequently the universal mission of the Church are of fundamental importance. The Church is therefore obliged to view evangelization to Jews, who believe in the one God, in a different manner from that to people of other religions and world views. In concrete terms this means that the Catholic Church neither conducts nor supports any specific institutional mission work directed toward Jews.[1]

This text clearly states that any institutionally planned missionary initiative toward the Jews is unacceptable. Of course, this does not prevent Christians from testifying to their Jewish brothers and sisters about their faith and coming to the belief that Jesus is the Messiah. The text in the same paragraph immediately follows: "While

---

1. Commission for Religious Relations with Judaism, "The Gifts and the Calling of God Are Irrevocable" (Rom 11:29): A Reflection on Theological Questions Pertaining to Catholic–Jewish Relations on the Occasion of the 50th Anniversary of *Nostra Aetate* (no. 4)," December 10, 2015, no. 40.

there is a principled rejection of an institutional Jewish mission, Christians are nonetheless called to bear witness to their faith in Jesus Christ also to Jews, although they should do so in a humble and sensitive manner, acknowledging that Jews are bearers of God's Word, and particularly in view of the great tragedy of the Shoah." This last reference to the Shoah is also remarkable and indicates the delicacy of this matter.

A Christian cannot question the universal salvific meaning of Christ. It is the heart of one's faith. Yet, at the same time, the Church believes that God has never broken God's covenant with Israel. God's calling and election are irrevocable. If we try to understand how the two can go together, we will probably never find a conclusive argument. We confront here the boundaries of theological reflection. But accepting those boundaries does not mean that we surrender to irrational and gratuitous insights. Rather, we are thrusting into the very secret of God's love and of God's plan of salvation for this world. God's ways are not ours and are ultimately unfathomable. Paragraph 37 of the same text of the Commission for Religious Relations with Judaism states that it "is not a matter of missionary efforts to convert Jews, but rather the expectation that the Lord will bring about the hour when we will all be united, when all peoples will call on God with one voice and 'serve him shoulder to shoulder'" (*Nostra Aetate* 4).

Of course, it is not the intention of this chapter to elaborate on the great importance of the dialogue between Church and Synagogue. We just wanted to show that pastoral and institutional missionary projects are not necessarily the obvious ways to bear witness to the gospel of God's love. In the case of Judaism, they are even inappropriate and anything but appropriate. The fact that the Jewish people remain part of God's plan of salvation for this world warns us against a one-sided ecclesiocentrism. God in Christ loved this world to the end. What God has begun, God will also complete. For that, God needs the Church. It is a visible and real sign of this as a sacrament. But it is not the Church but God who is and remains the actor of this redemption and no one else. And God knows ways to do so that we do not know. Nevertheless, a question arises here: Does what is said here about the significance of Judaism for the Church also apply to the other religions? Not in the same way. But can the other religions, and especially Islam, somehow be understood within God's plan of salvation of which Christ is origin and fulfillment? I do not have an answer to this question either. That is only possible if I also fully confess the uniqueness of Christ. But if it can be done, it will be in a way and along the ways that are only God's ways. As we read from Paul,

> What no eye has seen, nor ear heard,
>   nor the human heart conceived,
> what God has prepared for those who
>   love him.... (1 Cor 2:9)

The Second Vatican Council also explicitly states that "God's providence and God's proofs of goodness and decisions of salvation extend to all."[2]

It seems to me difficult, if not impossible, to deny the other religions any theological significance. I am thinking particularly of Islam: Muslims are believers in the true sense of the word, children of Abraham. From the perspective of the Christian faith, they can and should be approached and appreciated as such. But more broadly, all religions share in a common mission, each in its own way and from its own tradition, so that the question of what is beyond us humans and this world should not limit the question of the Absolute, the question of God. The meetings at Assisi that began on the initiative of John Paul

---

2. Pope Paul VI, *Nostra Aetate*, October 28, 1965, no. 1.

ll are prophetic in that sense. They demonstrate how much religions today are called to meet and appreciate each other, to pray and to work for a dignified society, for the preservation of creation and the salvation of all people.

That is why proselytism, as a method and as a strategy of missionary activity, is so reprehensible. Not only because of the lack of respect for the other person and his or her religious beliefs, but especially because it is assumed that I can indeed offer faith to the other. But I can't. I can testify to my faith. But it is only God who can open a person's heart. I have no power over any other human being.

If I want to make the gospel known to the other person, it can only be done in an encounter with the other person: an encounter worthy of the name, in which I meet the other person as another and recognize and appreciate him or her in being different. That is only possible if I have no plans in the back of my mind to make him or her "change his or her mind." When I want to meet someone with a different faith, not directly to convert them. I do it first based on the value of the encounter itself. I want to meet because he or she interests me and also because the faith of the other person fascinates me. It is because that encounter is important for my own search in faith. It can become a source of one's own deepening of faith. The proclamation of the gospel always presupposes that openness to the other. The other person is never just a passive receiver. Through the meeting, he or she becomes an interlocutor. It may always ultimately be the connection and friendship that evangelizes. As Paul VI so beautifully stated, "The Church must enter into dialogue with the world in which it lives. It has something to say, a message to give, a communication to make."[3] The Church herself becomes word, message, and dialogue.

An encounter does not happen with ulterior motives. An encounter does not find its meaning in function of anything else. It is its own meaning. I have nothing to sell and no product to put a price on. But it can happen, and it happens that the other person is touched by what I say or do and opens his or her heart. That is a miracle in every way. It is the work of God's grace.

---

3. Pope Paul VI, *Ecclesiam Suam*, August 6, 1964, no. 65.

15

The Spirit Who Is the Lord and Giver of Life

I N HIS SPIRITUAL testament, Christian de Chergé, prior of the community of Tibhirine, martyr who was beatified in 2018, refers to his meeting with Muhammad, a believing and devout Muslim. It was an encounter that fundamentally determined his life and vocation. He experienced that encounter as a great grace. In his own words, he writes, "It had been given to me to meet a mature man who liberated my faith." Christian was in Algeria from July 1959 to January 1961. It was the time of the Algerian war. Christian was still a seminarian. A close friendship developed between him and Muhammad. During a skirmish, Muhammed protected Christian. But the next day Muhammad was found murdered on the edge of a well. This Muslim gave his life for Christian. That's how Christian experiences it. And it is through Muhammad that Christian discovered and discerned his calling as a Christian monk. He became "one praying among other prayers." He renounced any desire to convert, he who received his own calling from Muhammad.[1]

In this act and in the death that followed, Christian recognized nothing but the gospel itself. It is the highest witness of martyrdom—a martyr of love. "No one has greater love than this, to lay down one's life for one's friends" (John 15:13). As the Church prays in the Eucharistic Prayer every time it celebrates the remembrance of Christ's great act of love, "When the Passover was imminent, his hour came. He had loved his people in the world. Now he gave them a proof of his love to the utmost." Without knowing it, Muhammad followed Jesus into giving his life. And Christian recognized Christ himself in this self-giving. Christian, who was preparing for the priesthood, discovered his vocation to monastic life. From

---

1. See Christian Salenson, *Prier 15 jours avec Christian de Chergé, prieur des moines de Tibhirine, Praying 15 Days Series* (Paris: Nouvelle Cité, 2006).

now on, he would always understand his vocation: "as one praying in the midst of other prayers."

I mention this gripping testimony here precisely to point out how much God is at work in the world. In John's Gospel, Jesus says, "Nevertheless I tell you the truth: it is to your advantage that I go away, for if I do not go away, the Advocate will not come to you. But if I go, I will send him to you" (John 16:7). And that Spirit was sent. This has been done in the power of the risen Lord. The resurrection of Jesus does not only concern him personally. Through his death and resurrection, the redemption of the world and of all creation has been definitively initiated. Nothing can separate this world from God's love. That does not depend on the expansion of the Church. It's not our job. It is and remains the work of the Spirit. That is what he was sent to do.

Like Christ, we also confess the Spirit as Lord and as the one who gives life: *Dominus et vivificans*— Lord and giver of life. The Church is a witness to the workings of this Spirit and may and must bear witness, in word and deed. The Church is the visible and real sign of this Spirit of love. Of course, that Spirit is at work in the Church; it is the Spirit who builds up the Church with a variety of gifts. But its action extends far beyond the boundaries of the Church. The Second Vatican Council explicitly states that God's grace is not only at work in those who believe in Christ:

> For since Christ died for all, and that the ultimate vocation of humankind is really unique, namely divine, we must hold that the Holy Spirit offers to all, in a way that God knows, the possibility of being associated with the paschal mystery.[2]

It is Karl Barth who pointed out that the application of the term *mission* to the Church only dates from the sixteenth century.[3] When the Church fathers and also medieval theologians spoke of mission, they always meant the *missio Dei.* By this was meant the mission of God: the mission of the Son through the Father and the mission of the Spirit through the Father and the Son. The Decree *Ad Gentes* of Vatican II also sees mission much broader than just the ecclesiastical mission.

> The pilgrim Church is by nature missionary, for it itself derives its origin, according

---

2. Second Vatican Council, *Gaudium et Spes*, no. 22.

3. Karl Barth, "La théologie et la mission à l'heure présente," *Cahiers du monde non chrétien*, 1932, no. 4, cited by Christian Salenson, *Christian de Chergé: Une théologie de l'espérance* [Christian de Chergé: A theology of hope] (Paris: Bayard, 2016), 212–13.

to the counsel of God the Father, from the mission of the Son and from the mission of the Holy Spirit.[4]

In its deeper sense, the term *mission* encompasses the entire redemptive work of God from creation to its consummation. If one sees mission exclusively as a mission of the Church, there is a danger that the Church will take the place of God. The success of the Church's mission is then easily and almost naturally confused with the Church's own territorial expansion. But mission is not the Church's job. It is God's work. The Church can and must participate in this work. However, not in every way. Only as a sacrament for this world. It is visible and an actual sign. The Church is a sign. But the *res sacramenti*, the way in which it is a sign, is God's work, the work of God's grace and God's great mercy for this world. The Church does not exist on its own. Not next to or apart from this world. It is not a separate world in itself. It does not live in opposition to the world. The Church can only understand itself in engagement with the world. Its mission can only be understood within God's history with the world, God's creation.[5] It

---

4. Second Vatican Council, *Ad Gentes*, no. 2.
5. See Salenson, *Christian de Chergé*, 212–13.

loses its purpose and meaning when it is no longer understood within the mystery of God's active and actual love for this world. It is that mystery that precedes all our works and all our pastoral work and of which we are not masters. The Church is the humble handmaid of God's plan of salvation that is beyond us.

In the First Epistle of Saint John there are these remarkable words: "Beloved, let us love one another, because love comes from God. Everyone who loves is born of God, and knows God. Whoever does not love does not know God, for God is love" (1 John 4:7–8). A little later, he writes, "God is love, and those who abide in love abide in God, and God abides in them" (1 John 4:16). It is striking that it is not said here that whoever does not love God does not know God. It does say that he who does not love does not know God. The love in question also concerns the love of one's neighbor. "Those who say, 'I love God,' and hate their brothers or sisters, are liars" (1 John 4:20).

What does this mean other than that one truly loves when one does not seek oneself nor one's own gain or profit but is committed to the happiness and well-being of the other. There God is truly present and God dwells in such a person.

God's life-giving Spirit does not work fruitlessly in this world. This is true even when one does not know or has not heard of God's incarnate Word and the Spirit that has come from Him and from the Father. We also sing it often in the liturgy: *ubi caritas et amor Deus ibi est* (Where charity and love reign, there is God).

The power of love that comes from God is expressed not just in the person-to-person relationship, it also plays a role in social relations, in political decisions, and in the formation of a human society. About Christ, who was appointed Lord by his resurrection and to whom all power has been given in heaven and on earth, the Second Vatican Council says,

> Christ is now at work in the hearts of men and women through the energy of his Holy Spirit, arousing not only a desire for the age to come, but by that very fact animating, purifying, and strengthening those noble longings too by which the human family makes its life more human and strives to render the whole earth submissive to this goal.[6]

---

6. *Gaudium et Spes* 38.

The Spirit is working within the circle of the Church, but also throughout the entire human family.

It is far from coincidental that in the liturgy, when the Church addresses its prayers to God, there is always prayer for those who rule us and for all those who bear great political and social responsibility, regardless of whether they are religious or not. One prays for them that they do not seek their own interests but always the common good. One prays that they work for a more just and humane society. One prays explicitly that God's Spirit may also be able to be over them and motivate them to promote humanity and solidarity worldwide.

In contrast to Eastern theology, the Holy Spirit in Western theology is often the great Forgotten One. This is not only so in theological reflection, but also in the experience of faith: not only in the personal experience of faith, but also in all questions about our presence in society and the relationship of the Church to the world. Nevertheless, the awareness of the worldwide action of the Holy Spirit for the salvation and redemption of all humanity is crucial to understanding our mission as a Church and our place in society. It is the belief that Christ did not die and rise in vain.

It is the belief that by the power of the Spirit he is truly working to save the world. Let us not forget the always surprising word of Jesus: "It is to your advantage that I go away, for if I do not go away, the Advocate will not come to you" (John 16:7).

That activity of the Spirit does not depend on the degree to which humans are aware of it. The Church is, of course, the community of those who are aware of this. That is the Church's great joy and the joy of every Christian: joy and gratitude that we have been given to have met Christ and to experience the power of his resurrection (see Phil 3:10). It is the joy to know that this world and all of God's creation are not doomed but destined for a new and incorruptible life. The joy to know that the Church may see the first signs of this, however small and sometimes hidden. They are signs of the breakthrough of God's reign, fruits of the Spirit, in her own midst, but also throughout the world. Even where we don't expect it. By contrast, "the fruit of the Spirit is love, joy, peace, patience, kindness, generosity, faithfulness, gentleness, and self-control" (Gal 5:22–23). They are so multiple and so liberating in all circumstances of life—in all our coexistence.

The Church lives in the changing of times. The Church knows good and bad days. Sometimes the Church lives somewhere in tribulation, while elsewhere the Church lives in very comfortable conditions. Sometimes it is very limited in its operation and is poor in people and resources. Sometimes the Church is a powerful institution, and sometimes a small herd. And sometimes it has also been the glorious Church. But periods in which the Church was held in high esteem and exerted much influence were not always and not necessarily the periods in which the Church bore the most witness to the gospel and in which the Church most testified to its calling as a sacrament of God's love for this world. They were strong shoulders that carried such opulence!

The circumstances and situations in which the Church fulfills its mission are therefore highly variable. But the meaning and the significance of the Church's calling and mission do not depend on these circumstances. It is not the circumstances that determine whether we as a Church respond to our vocation or not. Even if circumstances complicate the mission and make it less comfortable, that is no reason for despair. In the word of the Lord to Paul, "My grace is sufficient for you, for power is made perfect in weakness" (2 Cor 12:9).

This also applies to our time, when we as a Church live within the context of a secular culture.

We have come to see our relationship with society differently and to keep ourselves away from any form of conquest and patronage. We have become aware of our deep kinship with Judaism, living in deep communion with the Orthodox Church and with other Christian churches and communities—in sincere dialogue and friendship with the other religions and with all those who seek meaning and hope. We feel solidarity with all those who work in solidarity for a more humane society. Where we had initially come to see the changed time as a threat and hindrance, we have learned, as the Council has asked, to understand the signs of the times. God is able to make this time the time of God's grace.

CONCLUSION

IN THIS BOOK, I have reflected on the place and mission of the Church in a culture and in a society that are no longer religious or Christian in themselves. I want to end with some questions about the future of the Church. What is its future here in our regions? What will the Church and Christianity look like, here in the West, in fifty or a hundred years? Of course, no one knows. There are, however, trends that are becoming increasingly clear and that will probably determine the future. I will mention four of them.

The Church is becoming more and more a *modest* Church. That means a Church that accepts that it no longer has the social position it used to have. It is not a position where something is imposed on it against its will and that the Church is forced to accept, but a position that the Church itself wants and wholeheartedly endorses—accepting that the Christian faith is not socially evident, knowing that one does not represent everything and knowing that there are other options and possibilities. In other words, this means that the Church knows its place, in all humility, and should situate itself within the context of a modern, secular, and pluralistic culture.

The Church will also be smaller. I do not mean as a minority; but that could happen. It is not the case now. Christianity and the Church are too connected to the roots of our civilization and its historical and cultural heritage. In our society, Christians will remain a representative part of the population, just as Muslims are becoming. In addition to a more solid core, there will also be many who participate in the life of the Church in a differentiated way and do not want to break all ties with it. But the Church will no longer represent the vast majority in our society. It represents *a* point of view and *a* possibility. Knowing well and realizing that there are other points of view and other possibilities.

This will be most noticeable in the development of territorial pastoral care. In the past, it was the sign par excellence of a Church that was omnipresent and almost coincided with society itself. The Church occupied the entire terrain. The parish consisted of so many "inhabitants." But it has now become more than clear: the infrastructure we have inherited from the past no longer corresponds to the real position of the Church and Christianity in our regions. That is why the whole of Western Europe is in the process of restructuring territorial pastoral care. It's not about scaling up. Because even then, the logic of the occupation of terrain is still being considered. The main thing is that there are enough places of real Christian and ecclesiastical life with an outward appearance.

I expect the Church in the future to be more about professing—a Church that shows more clearly what it stands for and is not afraid of its individuality and identity. Precisely to the extent that the Church distances itself from any desire to Christianize society, the Church will inevitably be confronted more with the question of its true identity and its actual mission. It will be a Church that does not constantly seek to adapt its convictions to what is socially apparent today. In this sense, active societal pluralism is a very good thing. It is in the encounter with the other that I get to know myself, my otherness, and therefore my individuality.

This also applies to the Church. It is precisely in a secular and pluralistic culture that the Church knows that it no longer represents everything and everyone. It represents *a* point of view, *a* possibility. To be relevant, the Church must not limit its point of view to what are the general common concerns. In such a situation, the Church would pretend to still represent everyone. In this sense, too, the Church must be a modest Church: it is only what it is. But the Church is what it is! It is precisely for this reason that the Church will take greater care about its identity in the future; and the Church doesn't necessarily have to do that in a defensive position. It's just a matter of authenticity: honesty to oneself and to others. The Church must not pretend to be anything other than what the Church is. Only in this way will the Church also mean something to people who are searching in this secular culture and live with their existential and religious hunger. The truth remains: secular culture does not answer all questions, and it becomes dangerous if it pretends to do so.

I think the Church of the future must take great care of its own tradition and identity; and then, at the same time, it must remain an open Church. That is why Pope Saint John XXIII convened the Second Vatican Council. A Church that takes care of its identity, but at the same time closes itself off from the world, risks eventually behaving like a sect. Then it goes on the defensive against the world.

But the Church is not separate from the world, as Pope Francis constantly reminds us. The Church must not retreat into itself. The Church must not be merely concerned with its own inner church problems. The Church lives, with heart and soul, with the love and suffering of this world. The Church is open to searching people and truly welcomes them. The Church is also open to society, to this modern and secular culture. It is not judgmental and defensive, but lives in solidarity with the people of our time, with their hopes and their joys, with their sorrows and their fears. The Church participates in the social debates and is committed to a more humane world.

The opening words of the Constitution of Vatican II on the Church in the modern world, *Gaudium et Spes*, expressed it so movingly:

> The joys and the hopes, the griefs and the anxieties of the people of this age, especially those who are poor or in any way afflicted, these are the joys and hopes, the griefs and anxieties of the followers of

Christ. Indeed, nothing genuinely human fails to raise an echo in their hearts. For theirs is a community composed of men and women. United in Christ, they are led by the Holy Spirit in their journey to the Kingdom of their Father and they have welcomed the news of salvation which is meant for every human being. That is why this community realizes that it is truly linked with humankind and its history by the deepest of bonds.